Caught Reading Again

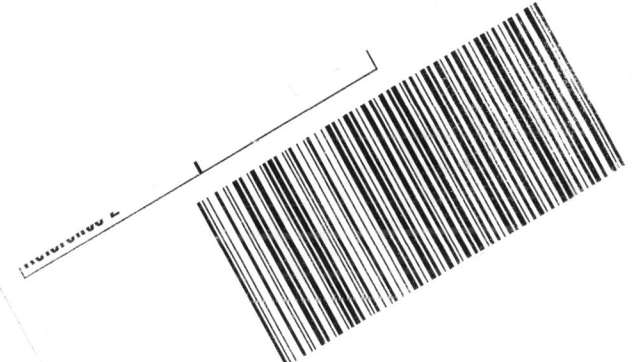

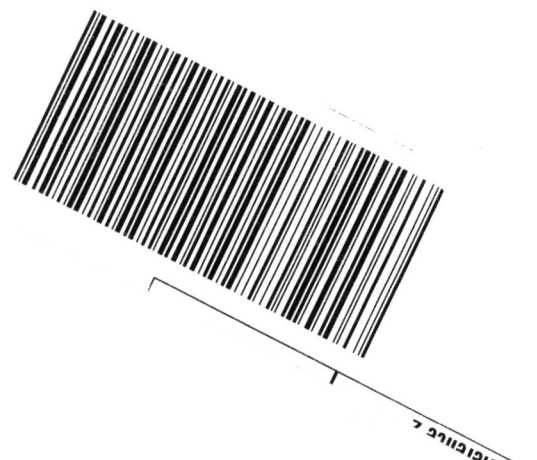

Caught Reading Again

Scholars and Their Books

Edited by

R. S. SUGIRTHARAJAH

scm press

© R. S. Sugirtharajah 2009

Published in 2009 by SCM Press
Editorial office
13–17 Long Lane,
London, EC1A 9PN, UK

SCM Press is an imprint of Hymns Ancient and Modern Ltd
(a registered charity)
St Mary's Works, St Mary's Plain,
Norwich, NR3 3BH, UK
www.scm-canterburypress.co.uk

British Library Cataloguing in Publication data

A catalogue record for this book is available
from the British Library

978 0 334 04109 2

Typeset by Regent Typesetting, London
Printed and bound by
CPI Antony Rowe, Chippenham SN14 6LH

Dedicated to

Marcella Althaus-Reid

(1952–2009)

Provocative thinker, daring theologian, a committed activist, an exemplary human being

CONTENTS

Part Two   Sense and Sensitivity: Theological Texts

CONTRIBUTORS

Marcella Althaus-Reid was Professor of Contextual Theology at the University of Edinburgh. She was a leading feminist and liberation theologian. Among her many publications are *Indecent Theology* (2000) and *From Feminist Theology to Indecent Theology* (2004).

Michael Amaladoss, from Tamil Nadu, India, is the Director of the Institute of Dialogue with Cultures and Religions, Chennai. He is also a professor of theology at Vidyajyoti College of Theology, Delhi. He is interested in the creation of an Indian theology and spirituality. His latest books include: *Living in a Pluralistic World* (2003), *The Asian Jesus: Making Harmony* (2007); and *Beyond Dialogue: Pilgrims to the Absolute*, forthcoming.

Roland Boer loves to travel by ship and cycle as far and as often as he can. He is also a research professor at the University of Newcastle, Australia, and writes in a number of different genres. His most recent publications are *Rescuing the Bible* (2007), *Criticism of Heaven* (2007), *Symposia* (2007), *Last Stop Before Antarctica* (2008) and *Political Myth* (2009).

Ada María Isasi-Díaz is Professor of Social Christian Ethics and Theology at Drew University in New Jersey. She has been an invited professor in Cuba, Korea and the Philippines, and lectures on justice as a reconciliatory praxis, the faith of the people as the source of theology, on religious understandings and practices of Latinas/os living in the USA, and on liberation perspectives in theology and ethics.

Lisa Isherwood is Professor of Feminist Liberation Theologies and Head of Theology and Religious Studies at the University of Winchester. She is an executive editor of the international journal *Feminist Theology* and has written or edited 15 books including most recently *The Power of Erotic Celibacy* (2006) and *The Fat Jesus: Feminist Explorations in Boundaries and Transgressions* (2008). She also likes golf and gardening, good food and company.

David Jasper is Professor of Literature and Theology at the University of Glasgow, where he founded the Centre for the Study of Literature, Theology and the Arts in 1991. He was the founding editor of the journal *Literature and Theology* and his recent publications include *The Sacred Desert* (2004) and *The Sacred Body* (2009). He is co-editor of the recent *Oxford Handbook of English Literature and Theology* (2007).

Kwok Pui-lan is William F. Cole Professor of Christian Theology and Spirituality at the Episcopal Divinity School, Cambridge, Massachusetts. She has always day-dreamed of becoming a writer. She enjoys reading widely outside her discipline and her most recent book is *Postcolonial Imagination and Feminist Theology* (2005).

Lesley Orr is a feminist historian, writer and activist, currently working at Scottish Women's Aid to develop the Scottish Government's strategy to address violence against women. She has taught practical theology, religious and gender history at the Universities of Edinburgh and Glasgow. Her publications include *A Unique and Glorious Mission: Women and Presbyterianism in Scotland c1830–c1930* (2000), and many articles on gender-based violence. Her current research interests include second-wave feminism and social change in Scotland.

Christopher Rowland is the Dean Ireland Professor of the Exegesis of Holy Scripture, University of Oxford. He has long-standing interests in the history of Christian radicalism and its relationship with apocalypticism. He is at present writing a book on the great English radical, William Blake's, biblical interpretation and on the influence of apocalypticism and mysticism on the New Testament.

Yvonne Sherwood is senior lecturer in Old Testament/Tanakh and Judaism at the University of Glasgow, Scotland. Previous publications include *The Prostitute and the Prophet* (1996; repr. 2004), *A Biblical Text and Its Afterlives: The Survival of Jonah in Western Culture* (2000), *Derrida and Religion: Other Testaments* (2004, co-edited with Kevin Hart) and *Derrida's Bible* (ed., 2004). She is currently writing a cultural history of the sacrifice of Isaac, concentrating on histories of secularization and ways in which the Bible has been politically and culturally reconfigured.

Daniel L. Smith-Christopher is Professor of Old Testament and Director of Peace Studies at Loyola Marymount University in Los Angeles. He works in multicultural and postcolonial interpretation of texts, and specializes in the Exilic and Post-Exilic periods of Old Testament History and Texts. His most recent works include *Biblical Theology of Exile* (2002), *Jonah, Jesus, and Other Good Coyotes: Speaking Peace to Power in the Bible* (2007). He also directs a Summer Study Abroad programme in New Zealand, and has a particular interest in the role of the Old Testament in recent and contemporary Maori culture and experience in Aoteoroa/New Zealand.

R. S. Sugirtharajah is Professor of Biblical Hermeneutics at the University of Birmingham. He has published extensively on the interface between postcolonialism and biblical studies. His most recent books include: *The Bible and Empire: Postcolonial Explorations* (2005) and *Troublesome Texts: The Bible in Colonial and Contemporary Culture* (2008).

Elaine Wainwright is Professor of Theology and Head of the School of Theology at the University of Auckland, New Zealand. She is a New Testament scholar and her research interests are biblical hermeneutics and contextual interpretations of scripture; her current research project being an ecological reading of the Gospel of Matthew. Workshops and seminars are among some of the ways in which she fulfils her commitment to making good biblical scholarship available to a wide audience.

Vincent L. Wimbush is Professor of Religion and Director of the Institute for Signifying Scriptures, Claremont Graduate University, Claremont CA. His research interests include the ethnographies and ethnologies of scriptures, with particular focus on the Black Atlantic. His most recent publication is *Theorizing Scriptures* (ed., 2008).

INTRODUCTION

Lost in Books

R. S. Sugirtharajah

What are you reading at the moment?
Alan Bennett, in *The Uncommon Reader*

'Tell me what you read and I'll tell you who you are' is true enough, but I'd know you better if you told me what you reread.
François Mauriac, quoted in Henry Hitchings, *How to Really Talk About Books You Haven't Read*

The idea for this volume came when I first read Anne Fadiman's *Rereadings,* in which 17 contemporary fiction writers revisit their favourite book, recollecting how they first read it and then explaining how they read the same text now. Re-reading a text that had made a tremendous impression leads them to talk about themselves, their personal and family lives, their prejudices and political views, and their literary ambitions and failures.

After reading Fadiman's book, I wondered whether we can come up with a similar book and invite some of the leading theological and biblical scholars to revisit the book/text that had a significant influence on their theological formation. The idea was to use the book as a device and ask the scholars to address the book's original context and its present status and standing: the memories these re-readings bring; the changed theological landscape; their theological and hermeneutical journey; their prejudices, theological likes and dislikes; and how these have shaped their professional life. What I had in mind was not a conventional book review as such, but an explanation of the relationship between the reader and the book, and an exploration of the question: do the book and the reader remain the same second time around? The volume in your hands now is the fruit of the scholars' intriguing re-encounters.

Volume: style and shape

As you will see, the authors I invited have come up with a variety of selections varying from secular to theological and biblical texts. Although these textual selections come out of different contexts, there is one common element that runs through the choice, namely the pervading influence of liberation hermeneutics. These essays roughly fall into two parts. Part 1, Meaning and Power: Political Texts, opens with Marcella Althaus-Reid's selection of a short story 'Evita Vive' by Néstor Perlonguer. She declares that the transgressive humour of this short story resonates more with Oscar Wilde than Gustavo Gutiérrez and its ideological thrust is closer to Queer literature than liberation theology. Michael Amaladoss has gone for the South Indian poet Subramania Bharathi, whose revolutionary poems stirred many Indian hearts during India's independence struggle. Roland Boer settles for Ernst Bloch's *Atheism in Christianity*, in which he discovered the Bible's continued appeal to revolutionary causes. David Jasper notes that his lifelong interest in and passion for theology and literature were inspired by reading Nathan A. Scott's *The Wild Prayer of Longing*. Scott was from a different racial and cultural background than David. His book, David came to see, anticipated many contemporary theological themes. Christopher Rowland recounts that it was the liveliness, militancy and resourcefulness of the seventeenth-century religion of England described in Hill's *The World Turned Upside Down* that led him to immerse himself in liberation theology and explore radical Christianity both in his writings and practice. For Vincent Wimbush, Olaudah Equiano's self-descriptive story, *The Interesting Narrative of the Life of Olaudah Equiano or Gustavus Vassa, the African* provides an opportunity to excavate, construct and communicate his own story. Daniel L. Smith-Christopher talks about how at a crucial juncture of his doctoral programme, his introduction to the work of anthropologist Nelson Graburn – *Ethnic and Tourist Arts: Cultural Expressions from the Fourth World* – helped him to rethink his views about biblical analysis and his perceptions of biblical texts as religious artefacts. R. S. Sugirtharajah narrates how accidentally discovering Said's *Orientalism* provided him with the hermeneutical tools which transformed his interpretative task.

The first three chapters which make up the second section – Sense and Sensitivity: Theological Texts – demonstrate how these essayists were heavily indebted to liberation hermeneutics. Both Kwok Pui-lan and Ada María Isasi-Díaz have chosen Gutiérrez's *Theology of Liberation*, a book which has effectively changed the way we do theology. Both recall with affection their indebtedness to and differences from the master's vision. Elaine Wainright recalls with fondness and gratitude Elisabeth Schüssler Fiorenza's *In Memory of Her: A Feminist Theological Reconstruction of Christian Origins*, a text which firmly stands within the liberative tradition but extends its scope to include the emancipatory concerns of women. It was this text which helped to mould Elaine Wainwright's theological thinking and brought home the important message of the public responsibility of biblical studies. The last two essays draw on biblical texts. Lisa Isherwood recalls her heightened perception of John's Gospel during her teen years and the marked impression it made upon her. Now, with hindsight, she concedes that the Fourth Gospel both facilitated and restricted her thinking. A similar experience is recounted in a jointly written piece by Yvonne Sherwood and Lesley Orr. This time it is the Old Testament book of Hosea. Yvonne Sherwood recalls how her childhood idea of God as love was affected when she became aware of the darker side of God as an abusive husband in Hosea. The book became more troubling when she read Lesley Orr's account of the contemporary testimonies of abused women who had been told by their abusing partners and by the clergy that their violation and entrapment had scriptural warrant in Hosea. This leads both of them to suggest that re-reading may no longer be an option.

As I write these summaries, an idea comes to my mind. What if this present exercise is reversed and these scholars were asked to revisit a book which in the early stages of their career they found annoyingly boring and thematically irrelevant? How would they now view a text in their mid or late careers, which was simply incomprehensible to their young minds?

Reading matters

People are drawn to books for reasons more complex than a simple love of reading. They stock their shelves with titles which tell the world who they are. The displayed books can be a reassuring sign of the journey one has made over the years. Books are seen as attractive and approved gifts. They can be regarded as the markers of good taste and bestow an element of self-importance. Books are still seen as a more trusted source than any other channel of information.

The entity which is known as the printed book is currently experiencing momentous modification. Technology is transforming our perceptions about books. With the introduction of electronic publishing, there will be three types of books – p-books (printed books), e-books (electronic books) and m-books (mobile books). The last one refers to cellphone novels – a new format which is becoming increasingly popular in Japan. According to media reports, half of the top ten Japanese novels were written for mobile phones. The electronic versions of the books will not provide the sensation of the smell of the page that we get when we flick through a brand new book. Where the printed book also scores over its electronic rival is that it lets one write in the margins. Those in the book trade say that an imaginative digital format has allowed the book to become more accessible to a new audience. Xeroxing replaced cyclostyling, and emails eclipsed the telegram, and the fear now is that the change from paper to pixels will result in the eventual demise of the printed format. Gail Rebuck of Random House reassures us that such a doom-ridden claim is exaggerated. She wants us to go beyond the restrictive binary type of thinking which pits e-books against p-books and to have a new conception of the book as a body of textual continuum which can be shaped and moulded into any number of formats. Common sense says there is room for both printed and electronic books. The perfect analogy is cinema and TV. Instead of finishing off the cinema, TV has co-existed with it, to their mutual benefit. Electronic publication in our discipline is still in its infancy. Cheaper production costs and market forces will compel theological publishing to go digital. I am longing for a day when I can carry 50 volumes of the sacred books of the East in my tiny palm.

Among the various human recreational activities, reading is widely held to be honourable and praiseworthy. Reading the latest literary or scholarly works marks you as an intelligent and a cultured person. In these days of mind-numbing TV programmes, any child found browsing in a book is likely to be proclaimed either precocious or talented. Books have become the measure by which most of us are judged to be either informed or inadequate. But such a view is not held by all. A recent survey conducted by the National Year of Reading Campaign and HarperCollins found among a certain class of people in the UK, namely lower-income and non-professional, that reading was seen as an activity of losers and books as 'acutely anxiety-inducing' and 'overwhelming'. What this group favoured and valued most was not such an isolating and sedentary pursuit as reading but communal enterprises such as DVDs and Wii games. There is a certain amount of snobbishness about reading. But books are no longer the sole site of information and entertainment. There are other compelling ways of spending one's time and learning about life and being entertained. Some people are not into reading as others are not into golf. In truth, what attracts people to books can now be supplied more quickly by information technology. Google, Wikipedia, YouTube and MySpace are all slowly emerging as providers of knowledge and information. Print culture is being slowly overtaken by digital culture. Proficiency in reading is essential to get along in life, for instance, for understanding instructions and regulations. But other skills also deserve our attention such as knowing how to fix a fuse or repair a defective cistern.

Honouring an unusual theologian

I end on a sad note. While I was in the process of editing this volume, the shocking news came of Marcella Althaus-Reid's death. Her essay in this volume must be one of her last writings. Ironically, hers was the first to arrive. Among the current crop of theologians, she was one of the most original and daring. It was she who audaciously asked how theology would look if Argentinian women did their theology without underwear. She was effortlessly capable of dealing with Fanon, Foucault, Said, Gutiérrez and Marx in one sentence. She was equally capable of turning liberation theology, feminism, Queer theory, post-structuralism and postcolonialism into a persuasive and explosive mixture. She was always a popular figure at international conferences, and one of the few theologians who had her own cult following. The enthusiasm and passion with which she conveyed her ideas will be hard to emulate. She has been an inspiration to many, and I hope the writings she left behind will inspire others.

Reference

A. Fadiman (2005), *Rereadings: Seventeen Writers Revisit Books They Love*, New York: Farrar, Strauss and Giroux.

Part One

MEANING AND POWER: POLITICAL TEXTS

I

WHEN THE GODS OF THE POOR REFUSE TO GO AWAY

Reading 'Evita Vive'

Marcella Althaus-Reid

> Y yo le pregunté si eso era una manifestación o un entierro . . .
> (And I asked if this was a political demonstration or a burial . . .)
> Néstor Perlongher, 'El Cadáver' (1980)

When did I first read Néstor Perlongher's short story 'Evita Vive' ('Evita Lives')? It is difficult to say. I knew the story through friends who by word of mouth retold the narrative of 'Evita Vive' during the time of its prohibition. It was published originally in what in Argentina we called 'counterculture' magazines such as *Cerdos y Peces* (*Pigs and Fishes*) in the 1980s and a few years later in *El Porteño*. The story, by the way, was written in 1975 during the highest point of the military dictatorship in Argentina. No wonder that it had already appeared in an English translation before it passed the severe censorship of my country.

When the story first appeared in Buenos Aires, I hurried to get a copy before the issue of *El Porteño* containing it could be recalled from the streets: such was the havoc created by what was considered the most scandalous, pornographic, almost sacrilegious story ever published. In fact, the journalists writing for *El Porteño* received death threats and the building was searched for bombs. *El Porteño* was well known as a leftist publication which never lacked courage at a time when death was the cost of truth and journalistic integrity. It was part of a group of courageous publications which sustained monthly critical reviews of the dictatorial regime of the 1970s in Argentina, at a time when the media were under severe control. But journals such as *El Porteño* did much more than criticize. Not only did they denounce the fascist government in power, they also published excerpts from banned books and writers. The censorship of books was not only political, but also ecclesiastical in a country where Church and State had very close interests and alliances of power. The condemnatory phrase used to justify the censorship of writers was to call them subversive 'terrorists and atheists'.

I am recalling here a time in the life of my country when I searched bookshops in vain for a copy of Rousseau's *The Social Contract* and was unable to order Paulo Freire's *Pedagogy of the Oppressed* from abroad. None of the important bookshops of the time wanted to get involved in such subversive material: it could have led to their names being added to the list of those suspected of terrorism. It was in this context that the journal *El Porteño* published Perlongher's story. It is a story which belongs to a genre illustrative of that humour, political and religious, which somehow characterizes Buenos Aires and its people. It is a sense of transgressive humour which has always been more in tune with Oscar Wilde than with Gustavo Gutiérrez, nearer to Queer literature than to liberation theology.

In those dark years of the Cold War and political persecution, cartoonists and writers in the Queer genre of ironic, if sometime melancholic, stories such as 'Evita Vive' provided a much needed quasi-spiritual horizon for a nation searching for the possibility of an alternative, in politics, social life and religion. Unfortunately, the price paid for circulating stories such as 'Evita Vive' was high. Perlongher himself was just one of the many authors who had to leave Argentina and go into exile: he was still a young man when he died some years later in Brazil.

The context: reading forbidden texts in the Bar La Paz

So it was that I had already heard of 'Evita Vive' before having the opportunity to read it: more importantly I already knew of this Queer writer called Néstor Perlongher years before having the opportunity to read anything by him. In my youth, in conversations during the wee small hours in the Bar La Paz in Corrientes Street, Buenos Aires, Perlongher's name was mentioned even though his works were not easily available. The mere mention of this writer's name was a subversive act, disrupting military and ecclesiastical control. Perlongher's name was itself a transgression. Together with other 'damned' writers from Argentina, such as Alejandra Pizarnik, Perlongher belonged to a group of notoriously defiant and creative writers. They were portrayed by the media as immoral, as enemies of the 'Western Christian Order' to which Argentina supposedly belonged. He was a gay activist, a politically critical voice and a devoted member of the Brazilian cult of 'Santo Daime', with its rituals of drinking traditional Amazonian hallucinogenic drugs. All this at a time when to overstep the horizon of the powerful state church guaranteed only trouble, political and religious.

Perlongher was a writer who seemed to have attracted a multitude of marginal identity markers. He was a gay activist, politically minded and an anthropologist – at a time when the study of anthropology was a career frowned on by the government. His stories contain strong sexual language (slang) and he died of AIDS. His questionings of the standards of sexual normalcy imposed by the dictatorial regime were linked to his criticism of fascism. He was a writer at the time when lists of forbidden texts accumulated daily in the national index of censorship. His works were burnt in strange company: books by Foucault and the Latin American Bible, the works of Freire and Nietzsche, the poems of Pablo Neruda. The list extended to high school texts on modern mathematics. They were all considered to be in one way or another terrorist in nature.

'Evita Vive': a first reading

When I say that 'Evita Vive' can be considered a sacrilegious text, I am referring to issues of spirituality among the poor. There were genuine spiritual elements in the relationship between Eva Perón and a particular generation of Argentinian people. They experienced profound transformation in their lives through her policies of welfare, they and the generation of their children. In the same way that Pentecostal people gather together to pray to the Holy Spirit for healing miracles, so the Argentinian poor gathered to give thanks for the miracles performed by Evita, programmes of welfare and equality previously unknown, from protecting the rights of workers to the right of women to vote. She was a politician who could change things and her subsequent holiness did not come from medieval miracles so close to the heart of the Vatican, such as statues which cry or walk, or a cough cured without antibiotics. She personified a civic call to sanctity. After she died and Perón was deposed, Evita's name could not be spoken in public. That was added to a colonial pedagogical system of forgettable knowledge to which people responded, not with names but with a national *imaginaire* of disappeared bodies.

When Perlongher wrote 'Evita Lives', it was not only living people who disappeared from their neighbourhoods as part of the communist witch-hunt. Tragically, corpse after corpse also disappeared without a trace, leaving only speculation about their fate. However, just as Evita's corpse disappeared from her grave for several decades, so these bodies never disappeared entirely from the public imagination. People keep exhuming them, either by making them wandering souls or, in the case of the Mothers of May Square, maintaining them as permanent reminders of the claims of social justice. 'Evita Vive' represents this spirit. It is a story about a quasi-resurrection (or exhumation) which involves Evita but also much more than her. Let us now consider the story.

The story: public sex

For those unfamiliar with Perlonguer's text, it can be introduced briefly by following the three scenes into which the story is divided. The story is difficult to translate, because of Perlongher's use of slang and the Queer riddle of his grammatical sentences. In fact, it is also a difficult and very ambiguous text to read, as it admits different interpretations. That textual ambiguity was emotionally uplifting for many readers, those of us who were at the time subjected to the almost canonical rules of approved understanding of life issued by the military regime.

The story line of 'Evita Vive' is as follows. The narrator's voice is that of a man called 'Chiche'. 'Chiche' is an old-fashioned nickname in Buenos Aires which can be applied both to women and to men. 'Chiche' (meaning 'little toy' or 'precious') sounds funny or camp, but also includes a class element. It is a nickname used among poor urban people. In this case, Chiche is a poor gay man from the docks, working in male prostitution: he first appears as a transvestite but later on it will look as if s/he is bisexual. Chiche has something to tell the reader, as a Queer raconteur of old and dangerous memories, concerning strange things that happened years ago. It involves the memory of three possible sexual encounters between Chiche and Evita – almost 30 years after her death.

In the first encounter, Chiche tells us about an incident involving his partner, a sailor called El Negro. The name, literally 'the black man', is a very masculine nickname of endearment in Argentina. El Negro was making love to a woman, or perhaps a transgender, in her/his own room. This scene took place in the boarding house room in the docks which he shared with El Negro. Chiche's anger, provoked by jealousy, is aroused but quickly resolved as the woman/transgender befriends him and they decide to share their mutual lover. The woman/transgender asks Chiche, 'Don't you recognize me?' Chiche realizes that she may be Evita. This is a line that in different ways will be repeated during the whole story, stressing recognition and remembrance. I read this as if Perlongher was asking me throughout the whole story, 'Have you yet forgotten me (Evita)? Have I changed so much?' The resurrected Jesus of the gospel came to confront those who had deserted him: do they love him? So here Evita, at home among the people of the docks, adopts a Queer gospel form of interrogation: do they love her, those who had benefited so much from her care for them? Years later, I would reflect theologically on the possibility of recognizing Christ not in a man, but in a woman. And not in any woman, but in an ultimately marginalized one, a prostitute woman from an urban city, abused, ill, living in poverty and loneliness. It is in that way that the transcendent meaning of God incarnates in history, and in the history of the marginalized, becomes revelatory.

That is one of the important aspects of the story, the sense of spirituality experienced at the margins among the dispossessed in Argentina by the name 'Evita'. Evita means solidarity and social justice but also love. No wonder my aunts had paintings of the Virgin Mary with Evita's face. She represented Christian virtues in a political life, but also a social discourse based on tenderness. Liberation theologians would later develop this combination. Perhaps that was the moment when the poor in Argentina sensed the meaning of an 'option' taken for them for the first time.

Was that woman kissing El Negro really Evita? It does not seem so. This is not a ghost story, and therefore the reader somehow knows she cannot be Evita. The points leading to the bodily identification of Evita in the story are always vague. They refer to her bleached chignon which appears dirty, how it might have looked when the embalmed body of Evita was interred. There are references to smells, reminiscent of a corpse or decay. There is also some skin discolouration, identified in the narrative with cancer, the illness that killed Evita. But if this is supposed to be a resurrection of Evita, it does not look like a rising to full glory in the afterlife. It is not a resurrection of monarchic ecclesial traditions, rather a resurrection of old ideals of social justice and love which a fascist dictatorship wanted people to forget. And these ideals are resurrected not in the episcopal councils or in cathedral Masses but at the margins of poverty and sexuality. Ideals resurrected among people struggling to survive and love in difficult times, without a God in heaven or a church on earth to protect them.

The Argentinian narrative of the disappearance of Evita's body after her funeral has always been highly religious. Those of my generation, for instance, recall a curious sequence. The military continually moved the corpse from one flat to the other and from an attic to a basement. But wherever it was taken in secret, within a few days candles would be lit outside, some flowers were laid and religious emblems appeared on the walls of the buildings. The military had to recognize that at least some people knew that the body was there: and so it was moved again. In Roman Catholic Argentina all this produced a deep spiritual crisis. The body was not interred and there was uncertainty about what had happened to it. Stories circulated claiming that the corpse had been raped, mutilated, burnt or thrown into the River Plate. Evita could not rest in peace. Yet there was a further confusion. In Argentina, every dead person contributes economically to the Church by the fact that the family pays for many Masses for the salvation of the soul of the departed. Yet, here the Church itself participated morally in this religious scandal of condemning a soul to a wandering existence. The faithful were astonished. Yet, the poor, in the midst of their difficult, vulnerable lives, still asked this soul of Evita, this soul exiled from political spaces below and heavens above, to intercede for them.

This first scene ends with 'Evita' asking Chiche to go to heaven with her, because there are lovely guys there. The scene is camp, but political too. Evita shows sadness in saying that nobody can trust the love of sailors nor the love of army generals, those generals who betrayed Perón after her death. At the end, Evita gave Chiche a handkerchief embroidered in gold. Chiche lost it, as someone (one of many lovers) took it away with him.

This first part of the story produces mixed feelings, the kind of feelings that should not be mixed in a decent society, feelings of promiscuity and friendship, political criticism and sexual orgies. Perlongher made the private public: public sex with Evita among the sexually marginalized becomes a sign of the deconstruction of the political and ecclesial 'decency' systems of the military regimes. Just as with de Sade, Perlongher's revolutionary protest comes dressed in sexual excess. But there is much more to his writings than that.

Second scene

After this first act of encounter with a supposed Evita, the second scene of the story takes us to another boarding house, or perhaps even a *conventillo*. These were old-fashioned compounds where poor immigrants traditionally rented rooms, frequently owned by the Catholic Church. Generally they consisted of a large patio, perhaps with trees, surrounded by rooms for rent and providing one or two communal toilets and a public tap for water. In this part of the story, Perlongher describes how a group of Queer people are having a noisy party in which sex and cannabis are the main ingredients. This suggests a decadent, sexually excessive scene. The police intervene, to seize people and take them off to jail, but at this point, the story takes a significant twist. A woman or transvestite at the centre of the party challenges one of them: 'You, beast (*pedazo de animal*), how are you going to take Evita to jail?' The response is silence and the faces of the policemen grow pale at the mention of the name. The effect is similar to that in the first scene: 'Do you know who I am?' The woman speaks, breaking the silence: 'No, let everybody listen now . . . Now, you want to take me to jail, when 22 or 23 years ago, I brought a bicycle for your kid to your home . . . ' Such an action, incidentally, was an emblematic characteristic of Evita, as the giver of presents to the poor who visited her at the Ministry of Social Work during her lifetime. She sent bicycles to kids and sewing machines to their mothers. During the time that Perlongher wrote this story, it was said that the guerrilla movement was made up of those children from poor families who received gifts from Evita.

However, the scene deteriorates in such a camp way that there is no doubt that this is a complete parody. One laughs out loud while reading the text. Only a group of simple, working-class policemen could have doubts. Or rather not doubts, but an emotional confusion provoked by the memories of Evita as an agent/angel of social justice. But my laughter was suddenly interrupted by a different scene, one which I consider deeply moving. As the confusion gives place to more scenes of sexual debauchery, someone shouts, '*Muchachos* (lads), they are going to take Evita to jail!' This is followed by some paragraphs which were to influence my spirituality for years to come, which made me receptive to liberation theology in my mid-twenties.

The irruption of the poor

At that point in the narration, when the camp phrases and the fun of misinterpretations and sexual excesses becomes hilarious, the scene changes. The people living in the rented rooms, the poor and the elderly, appear on the scene. They have heard that Evita was going to be taken to jail and they have come, ready to fight for her. One old lady shouts, 'Evita has come from the Heavens!' This is a historical parody. It recalls the *coup d'etat* of 17 October 1945. The military had closed the bridges leading to Buenos Aires, but the workers swam across the river to reach the city, in response to the call of Evita to defend the government. At the time, the media referred to this multitude of workers who poured on to the streets to defend democracy as 'a presence from the zoo' (*aluvión zoológico*). If the word 'zoo' originally denoted strange forms of life, then the crowds were indeed from the zoo, from the margins of society, those excluded by the State and the Church. This was an irruption from the poor, the visible presence of those normally hidden away, and the vulnerable presence of the wretched of history: yet there was something spiritual moving among them. They followed 'Evita' as orphans of a wandering nation in exile from a land of social justice and solidarity and asked her not to abandon them. 'Evita' then turned towards them and addressed them as historically Evita had done so often in the past, as *Mis grasitas. Grasa* was a term of dismissal applied to the poor, but Evita turned it into a term of endearment. The discourse continues. Evita needs now to return to heaven, but she knows everything and from there she will protect her people from any evil. The poor people cry out. Evita is that ubiquitous divinity of the poor, all bountiful but impotent, not a God of the margin but the ultimate marginalized God.

All the names are false

The third and final scene of the story is situated in the streets of Buenos Aires. Several years later a mysterious woman, in a chauffeur-driven car, picks up Chiche from the street, offering money for sex. In the darkness of the tinted windows of the car, Chiche cannot be sure about her identity and yet she seems familiar. Chiche seems now to be more a male prostitute than a *marica del Puerto* or a festive transgender fighting for a sailor lover. The mysterious woman is identified by Chiche as 'a real woman' and a desirable one. Later, in the intimacy of her room, the question of recognition will come again. The body identifications from the first scene are re-enacted: the faded blonde chignon, the skin discolourations and the odd smell of decay, as with a corpse. Chiche tells how, before leaving the room, he stole a pearl necklace from her, which he then attempted to sell. He cannot say, at this point, if the woman who paid him to make love to her was Evita or not. However, the pearl necklace is a silent witness. Chiche is arrested when attempting to sell a historic necklace which did indeed belong to Evita Perón.

The final words from Chiche are mysterious. Once the police have become involved, things seem dangerous. So Chiche addresses his street gang (gays/trans-prostitutes?) and the whole gang decides to disappear from the street where they used to gather. As used here, the verb 'to disappear' is a highly charged metaphor, politically speaking. But more widely, the whole story is a hide-and-seek narrative between the dead and the living and between the abandonment of the people from the margins by their divinities and their presence as marginal gods. And so they left their habitual gathering in that street, Chiche remarks, for it had become dangerous. Chiche's final words do not bring the story to a close, but rather leave it open for ever, as if in waiting for a final resurrection of Evita that will never fully happen, yet it is already among us. So Chiche assures us that all the names in the story have been changed.

But of course this is a story about a name, as in the Bible, a name which cannot be pronounced, a name whose reality evades us even if we speak it. If all names in the story are false, 'Evita Vive' is not about Evita living. What then is the story about? This is a story about the gods of the poor and the marks they leave in history. This is a parable about the search for those signs.

Gods of the poor

I rebel with indignation . . . against the privileges of the army and the clerical forces . . . But I also know that people are repelled by the arrogance of the military who think that they can monopolize the [idea of the] nation. And I also know that people cannot reconcile the humility and poverty of Christ with the fatuous arrogance of ecclesiastical dignitaries who think that they can monopolize religion. The nation belongs to the people, the same as their religion. (Eva M. Duarte de Perón, 1952: 14)

The first time that I read Gustavo Gutiérrez (and José Maria Arguedas, the Peruvian novelist who was Gutiérrez's friend and inspirer), I remembered my first reading of 'Evita Vive'. Behind Gutiérrez's passionate plea for the poor there are also strong emotions for this destitution of God in Latin American history. Those are emotions of anger but also of compassion and tenderness. 'Evita lives' not only because people's own sense of social justice lives but because God leaves marks and signs of God's own presence amidst destitution and vulnerability. And Perlongher has succeeded in putting together a track of spirituality and the categories of marginalization of his story, just as the Gospel writers succeeded in making of Jesus the ultimate marginalized, a victim who attracted all kinds of violence against him. The context of 'Evita Vive' sets transgression at exemplary levels, for not only is this a story about the coming back of a forbidden political name, but also of the whole ghost of the military Junta. It is the ghost of the Peronist project of social justice and welfare system, represented, in one of the most patriarchal countries of South America, in the figure of a young woman politician. And a woman who stood as an illegitimate daughter (or 'daughter of sin' according to the legislation of the times), therefore suffering legal discrimination. All this and much more is represented in the name 'Evita' for the Argentinian reader. It is a name representing a denunciation against a wealthy church and its privileges, a church which has subjected the gospel to political pacts and worldly power and also a church which has set the codes of decency/indecency which seemed to found the moral values of the criminal juntas.

Therefore Perlongher's search for testing the ways of transgression is exemplary, for he discerned the links between the normalization of sexual ideologies and the violence of hegemonic political claims. Yet in the midst of the struggle for survival among the poor of the poor, who statistically in Argentina have been the transgender people, there are spiritual signposts represented in Queer desire among the structures of death prevalent in the country. There is a desire for life, abundant, promiscuous and growing outside containers, a desire for a meaningful life which would include the instability of ambiguous hermeneutics and a kernel of social justice as the privileged communion between the poor and their gods.

Spirituality, poverty and sexuality

Two decades later I found myself re-reading 'Evita Vive', this time in the English version, to a group of British friends. They were acquainted with the Latin American genre of magical realism and yet they found this story shocking, almost obscene. How could I find spirituality, they asked me, when they could only see gay prostitution, camp mockeries scenes and orgies? Something similar has happened to me when I have tried to share the words of some very old, traditional tangos from my country. Wherever I was touched by stories of the struggle of poor women in the words of the tango and praised their courage in adversity and the social denunciation of injustices, my friends saw only their promiscuity: moral condemnation disqualified their prophetic voices. In 'Evita Vive' the category of the narrator ('Chiche') as a promiscuous gay, transgender or bisexual is probably one which European readers may identify only as a prostitute, or in any case, its identity will be primarily sexual. However, when I read the story I simply identified him as a survivor of difficult political, religious and economic circumstances, with whom I had an immediate sense of solidarity. The same response is elicited with respect to some tangos. In these the words clearly refer to women prostitutes from a mythical beginning of the century in Buenos Aires. Where I came from they attracted only feelings of sympathy, the feelings of solidarity which inform the critical realism of the community of the poor in any large Latin American city. More than sympathy, it is the spiritual experience of finding God, that biblical God of the mountains who appeared with clouds and thunder as the God of transgressions, except that this time the smoke and lightening were associated with the stubborn contradiction between the legislation of life and its suppression through necrophilic political structures.

A few years ago, as I stopped to listen to the sound of drums and the songs coming from a public demonstration of workers in Buenos Aires, I remembered Perlongher. Later, when I saw the cathedral of Buenos Aires sprayed with graffiti defying the Church for the politics of civic (not just religious) discrimination and hate against gays in Argentina, I remembered Perlongher. I also remembered Perlongher in the AIDS rallies and in the *escraches* or public demonstrations that the children of the disappeared organize against the torturers who still live comfortably in Argentina. Even the films of Almodóvar remind me of Perlongher's 'Evita Vive'. There too we find that solidarity of the marginalized, the Queers and homeless people, the women who have survived abuse and the multitudes of people who in the eyes of the market society are failures. Together they have many spiritual lessons to teach a church which has imprisoned God in its own construction of decency. That decency is not a theologically or ecclesiastically neutral term but an ideologically charged one, based on classist, racial and political interests. Promiscuity or sexual practices outside the ideology of heterosexuality are considered scandalous, but the Argentinian church was not scandalized by persecution, torture or economic corruption, nor did it publicly condemn such practices. Public sex was a sin, but the private acts of destroying people's bodies in concentration camps were not an issue for the confessional. For that reason, 'Evita Vive' works as a powerful metaphor of the lesser divine expectations of the lesser people. Through it the presence of God in the margins requires us to consider the marginalization of God, or the irruption of God among them. Those who have been considered ideologically too poor, too ignorant or too far outside the regimes of sexual (hetero) normality, prophetically convey to us in this story of Perlongher the meaning of the irruption of a God whose capacity to transgress our regulatory systems of love has never ceased.

References

N. Perlongher (1980), 'El Cadáver', in *Austria-Hungría*, Buenos Aires: Tierra Baldía.
N. Perlongher (1997), *Prosa Plebeya*, Buenos Aires: Colihue.
Eva M. Duarte de Perón (1952), *Mi Mensaje*. Available online, http://www.emancipacion.org/libros_revistas/MiMensaje.pdf

2

SUBRAMANIA BHARATHI

Michael Amaladoss

One of my memories as a small boy is the singing of patriotic songs by Subramania Bharathi (1882–1921). World War Two was in its final years. The freedom movement in India under the leadership of Gandhi was very active. An unforgettable event was my having a glimpse of Gandhi as he was looking out of the window of his railway compartment when his train stopped for a few moments at a local railway station near our village. I was perched on the shoulders of my father. My father, a teacher, was an ardent follower of Gandhi. So we used to take part in processions and meetings of the freedom movement. They always included songs of Bharathi. I learnt them from others and sang them with gusto. India became independent in August 1947 and in June that year I entered a Jesuit boarding school. Both events contributed to the temporary disappearance of Bharathi from my horizon. His songs and poems had not yet got into our textbooks of Tamil literature.

My first serious acquaintance with Bharathi

I began reading seriously and with interest the poems of Bharathi only in my college years. I was already a Jesuit and we were interested in discovering our Indian identity and our roots in Tamil culture. As Christians, we had been a little alienated from them. This was my first introduction to Bharathi as a poet. I now read the national songs that I had only heard and sung in my childhood. Besides these, Bharathi had also written many other songs and poems. A standard collection of his poems contained in a first part national songs, devotional songs, wisdom songs, and miscellaneous songs. The second part included four longer pieces: his autobiography, songs on Krishna, a small narrative on the 'Vow of Panchali' taken from the *Mahabharatha* and a novelette called the 'Song of the Cuckoo'. Bharathi also started a new era in Tamil poetry. The language is simple and easily accessible to everyone. The rhythms lend themselves to song. Though he wrote largely in traditional metric verses, he also experimented with 'prose poems'. For much of his life he was an active journalist. For some years, he had to take refuge in Pondicherry, a French colonial enclave within Tamil Nadu.

When Bharathi wrote his national songs the freedom movement had started, and was slowly catching fire. The quest for freedom from British colonialism underlay all the songs, finding open expression in some of them, exhorting people to courage in conflict. Some of the songs are in praise of various national leaders. The freedom movements in other countries such as Italy, Belgium and Russia are also evoked. Supporting this general theme of freedom are others, such as feeling proud of the natural and cultural riches of the nation and the need for social and economic reform. The mountains and the rivers, the rich human resources, the various literary and cultural achievements, the deep religiosity, the enterprising cultural and trade missions to foreign countries, the beauty and energy of its people are all listed with rich imagination and poetic grace. The nation is seen as the mother and divinized, adding a spiritual dynamism to the freedom movement. We owe our mother devotion and loyalty. We need to restore her glory which has faded under foreign domination. At the same time there are social diseases from which she needed to be cured: economic disparities and exploitation, the divisive caste system, the oppression of women, various superstitions and illiteracy. Some phrases have become popular slogans.

> If there is no food even for an individual, we will destroy
>   the earth!
> If there is true light in the heart, it will enlighten one's
>   speech!

We will be slaves to no one on this earth. The Lord alone
will we serve!
Among the languages we know there is none as sweet as
Tamil!
There are no castes; it is sin to speak of inferior and
superior people!
Let us burn the foolishness that depreciates women![1]

Another important group of his songs are devotional. There
are songs on all the popular gods of Hinduism. But the prin-
cipal focus is on the mother goddess, *Shakthi* or Energy. She
is the formless behind all the forms, the origin and goal of all
things. The vision is *advaitic* or non-dual. She energizes and
evokes a lot of emotional devotion and commitment. In the
Hindu pantheon she is the consort of Shiva. Another divine
image that attracts considerable attention is Krishna. He is the
avatar (manifestation) of Vishnu who helps the Pandavas in
battle in the great epic *Mahabharatha*. More particularly he is
the hero of the *Bhagavad Gita* or Song of the Lord, which is a
kind of gospel for modern Hindus. In this, he urges Arjuna, the
warrior, to fight on behalf of justice, setting himself as a divine
example. Both Shakthi and Krishna evoke a fighting spirit,
standing up for justice and freedom. At the same time they
also make it a spiritual experience of cosmic communion, with
the nation mediating the Absolute. There is also another twist.
Krishna (Kannan in Tamil) is also evoked in the female form of
Kannamma. As a matter of fact the 'Songs on Krishna' evoke
Krishna as lord and servant, father and mother, bridegroom
and bride, guru and disciple, child and friend (playmate).
Krishna as Kannamma may symbolically merge with Shakthi.
Bharathi's vision of Shakthi as the cosmic, divine force also
enables him to see her as the one reality that manifests itself in
all the religions and therefore unites them as different expres-
sions or names of the one Truth. He says, for instance,

---

1 There are many collections of *Bharathi's Poems*. I am using the
Poombuhar Edition (Chennai, 2004). The translations are mine. For the
texts here, see pp. 44, 50, 62, 50, 222, 61. References hereafter will be
to this edition by page numbers.

The one who revealed the mystery to the prophet
  Mohammed,
The father of Jesus – various believers
Imagine the Transcendent and praise it in various ways;
It is one and its nature is enlightening knowledge;
Those who realize it are free of all suffering. (p. 218)

The wisdom and general songs deal with ethical themes
for children or occasional songs to honour various people or
events. The autobiography is actually a collection of reflections
on various themes. However, it does refer to the fact that he
was attracted to a girl, of a lower caste than his. But he was
not allowed to continue the relationship, leading to an early
marriage at the age of 14 with a girl aged 7. After the sudden
death of his father, he finished his studies in the north of India,
staying with his uncle in Varanasi, the centre of Hindu learning
and popular religiosity. There he acquired a working knowledge
of Hindi and Sanskrit. The justification he gives for writing the
'Vow of Panchali' is to introduce the epic of *Mahabharatha* to
the Tamils in an easily accessible diction. Looking at his poems
as a whole I can say that he is a modern Tamil poet, people oriented, nationalist and liberative, socially aware and revolutionary, and a mystic *bhakta* in the classical Tamil Hindu devotional
tradition. People consider him the best modern Tamil poet.

The context for re-reading Bharathi

I am now seriously re-reading the text after nearly 50 years.
Though India has been independent for 60 years, we seem still
to be living in an ambiguous situation. India is no longer a
political colony, but still remains an economic and perhaps
a cultural one. Economically India may be slowly emerging
into a certain independence. But culturally the Western media
dominate at least the elite, who, however, seem to have a love–
hate relationship with the West. One likes to be American, but
at the same time one also affirms one's Indian roots, though
in a selective manner. My part of India – Tamil Nadu – has
gone through a period of struggling for an independent iden-

tity and has now settled for an autonomous one, politically and culturally, built around the Tamil language. In the last two decades the subaltern groups like the Dalits have started to assert themselves. But poverty and social inequality persist in multiple ways. Caste groups are becoming political and inter-caste tensions are on the increase. A movement for the liberation of women has also become active, perhaps more in practice than in theory. With the rise of the Hindutva movement and the global affirmation of Islamic identity the relations between the religions have become tense. Much of this development can be considered postcolonial. The social divisions that were dormant or under control during the colonial period are now coming out. Society may be moving towards a new equilibrium. In the meantime this is a period of tension and search for identity. Reading Bharathi in this context, what are my reflections?

I know that grand narratives are not popular in the postmodern world. However, looking at Bharathi, I see an inclusive person at the cultural, social and religious level. Or looking from the other direction, I see him being comfortable with pluralism without any efforts to impose a dominating unity – from his own point of view. Being a poet, he felt at home with symbols and with the imagination. So he could feel at home with pluralism without being bothered by rational, universal concepts that discount it.

A broad nationalism

Bharathi's nationalism was broad and inclusive. At one moment he is praising the riches of Tamil and Tamil Nadu. In the next song, he will be glorifying the Indian nation, evoking its mountains and rivers, its glorious past rich in creativity and culture. He describes India as a mother through whom the divine Mother is operative. In his inclusive vision, distinctions, while real, are not divisive. He speaks of the Aryans and the Vedas as sources of Indian culture. For him, Indian culture and history are one-in-many. The Aryans and the Dravidians are one people, heirs to one composite culture. He condemns the evils of the caste system with its inequality. He asks for the freedom of the Dalits. At the same time, he seems to accept the caste system, as Gandhi did, as a social division of labour. His quest for freedom becomes global when he sings in praise of liberation movements in Russia, Italy and Belgium. He sees them all as related. But he is also aware of Indian women labourers being exploited in Fiji. The Tamils today, particularly the Dalits, will have difficulty in accepting his views. In Tamil Nadu today, Tiruvalluvar (third century BC?) is more popular than Bharathi, though no one will speak against Bharathi.

After Bharathi, Periyar came into Tamil Nadu politics. 'Periyar' means the 'great one', though his original name was E. V. Ramaswamy Naikar. He experienced the Tamils as being oppressed by the Aryans. The Aryans were identified as migrants from the north of India, whose original language was Sanskrit, and who systematically exploited and oppressed the poor people of the South in the name of caste, legitimized by Hinduism. By limiting education to themselves, the Brahmins also had an early start in profiting by the modern education system brought by the British and in cornering the jobs that were on offer. So he started a Dravidian movement that struggled for the identity and freedom of the Dravidian Tamils against the oppressive Northern Aryans. The oppression is, even today, religious and cultural rather than directly political. The Dravidian parties have been in power for over thirty years in Tamil Nadu. There was a separatist sentiment for some time which was abandoned later, probably with the division of the states according to language so that the Tamils now have their own state, which is relatively autonomous. I would say that the religio-cultural domination is still very much there, though somewhat hidden. Here we see Bharathi's view of the history and culture of India as a seamless unity opposed by Periyar's view of them as conflictual and oppressive. Though this desconstruction of history is bit simplistic, I think that it is basically correct. Of course, Bharathi, being a Brahmin (Aryan), would have been uncomfortable by such an interpretation of history. On the other hand, India has a certain undeniable geographical, cultural and even religious unity, whatever the conflicts and tensions through which it has grown. The growth has not been smooth. But it has rather been dialectical, giving and taking, as others like Ananda Coomaraswamy would suggest.

A similar tension would be present with regard to the caste system. There is no doubt that Bharathi was against caste inequalities. But no one would today accept the caste as simply a division of labour. One belongs to a caste by birth. Besides, the labour is not neutral, but graded in terms of purity and pollution, honour and dishonour. So a Dalit is born with a handicap that he may not be able to overcome. To restore social equality is not merely a question of changing minds, but also of changing social structures. Bharathi himself was personally beyond practising such social discrimination. But he was not able to change the structures. Today, there is a further twist. The Dalits want not only to be recognized as social equals, but to affirm their socio-cultural and even religious identity as different. Some Dalits today say that they are not Hindus. Others convert to Islam or Christianity. The government has a programme of affirmative action to help the Dalits rise educationally and economically. This is far from being fully effective, and socially it has made no difference. Only the people together can bring about change and I do not see many efforts being made towards this. The Dravidian parties do promote inter-caste marriages. That is certainly one sure way of promoting social equality since it dilutes the purity of blood. But this movement is not widespread. I think that in this matter Bharathi, if he were alive, would be more open and understanding.

In any case the dividing line is not between Brahmins and the Dalits, but Dalits and others. Not all Dravidians are Dalits. In Tamil Nadu, if the Dalits are about 18 per cent and the Brahmins about 4 to 5 per cent, that leaves nearly 75 per cent others. Contemporary Tamil culture is a joint product of the Dravidian and Aryan genius. Bharathi is a great modern Tamil poet even though he is a Brahmin. Tamil culture is not a monolith and today, not only the Dalits, but every caste is affirming its historical and cultural identity. At the same time, at the level of the media and literature the differences are not great. We are surely in for a period of churning. While differences should be accepted and respected, I do not think that fragmentation will help. India has a cultural and social unity that should not be abandoned, though imbalances should be corrected.

Today the Muslims and the Christians would object to Bharathi's divinization of the country, which links it too closely to the Hindu vision of the divine. They would rather affirm India as a secular, non-religious, political structure. They would not like to see it Hinduized. Recently there were protests, particularly from the Muslims, when one of the states of India obliged all the children in the schools to sing *Vandematharam* as a national anthem. Though this song has been recognized as one of the two national anthems, it is hardly ever used. The Hindutva party wanted to use it as a way of affirming India as Hindu since it divinizes India as a mother goddess. Bharathi offers two Tamil versions of the song and certainly agreed with its perspective.

An inclusive religion

Bharathi sings of and to many Hindu gods and goddesses. But he is a strong *advaitin* (non-dualist). For him, ultimate reality is One. His preferred symbol for this Ultimate reality is Shakti or 'energy', experienced as feminine. He may further identify it with Kali, the consort of Shiva. His devotion to this ultimate feminine is mystical. Once he realizes that the Ultimate is one, though it may have many symbols, it is only one step to say that the believers of other religions worship this same Ultimate through other symbols. I think that it is good here to make a distinction between a name and a symbol. Names are simple designations. A tree may be called by different names in different languages. A symbol, however, refers to a particular dimension or function or history of the thing symbolized. It is not very clear whether Bharathi made such a distinction. He sings, for instance:

On the earth, there are five continents, but religions are a crore!
Bhuddism, Jainism and the religion of the Parsees,
The religion that worships the feet of Jesus as Lord,

The eternal Hinduism, Islam and Judaism,
The well named Taoism of China,
The good Confucianism and so on – in the world
There are so many religions that I know;
But their meaning is one . . .
You are Lord; you are Lord; God are you;
Tatvamasi, tatvamasi, Thou art That![2] (p. 298)

Bharathi had contacts with Muslims and Christians in the country. As a matter of fact he has a song in praise of Jesus and another on Allah (cf. pp. 193–4). Gandhi had a similar inclusive vision.

The problem today is that whatever one may think about the oneness of the Ultimate at philosophical, spiritual and mystical levels, at the ordinary religious, historical and socio-political levels the religions *are* different. They are further hijacked by economic and political interests. There are fundamentalist groups in every religion. So we have to accept and respect these differences. All that we can hope for is that each religion is able to make space for other religions within its own tradition. Divisions between religions have become today international. It is perhaps significant that in a recent survey (September 2007), out of 70 countries surveyed, India was one of two countries where people were in favour of the US military presence in Iraq.

While we appreciate Bharathi's inclusive religious vision and desire that people belonging to different religions develop such a vision from the point of view of their own religion, in practice we have to accept that religions and religious communities are different. We have to avoid inclusive visions that tend to be dominant. Given the history of violence, we will have to promote forgiveness and reconciliation. But beyond that we need to encourage dialogue that can lead to mutual knowledge, understanding and enrichment. Gandhi has also initiated a tradition of common prayer. Basically we have to commit

---

2 *Tatvamasi* means 'Thou art That'. This is the basic affirmation of the *Upanishads*, that reality is one. 'Thou' – the *atman*, the self – art 'That' – the *Brahman*, reality. See also pp. 82, 119, 140, 151, 161 (Shakti is one and many) and so on.

ourselves to live as citizens of the same country and collaborate at the economic and political levels to build a better society for all.

Social reform

Bharathi speaks about the abolition of poverty, inequality and injustice (cf. pp. 44–5, 60 etc.). He does not go into structural analysis of society as Marxists might. But he has a deep desire for economic equality. He is particularly eloquent about the liberation of women (cf. pp. 226–31). He wants them to be educated and treated as social equals. But what is special about Bharathi is the link between his vision of the Ultimate as the feminine figure of Shakti and his respect for women. This regard is also shown in his imagination of Krishna as a woman. In the *Bhagavad Gita*, Krishna shows Arjuna his divine form embodying the whole universe. Bharathi imagines a similar embodiment, but it is the body of Kannamma (Krishna as a woman) (p. 164). I have not come across this in any other bhakti poets. He sees women themselves as images of Shakti. I have the suspicion that he writes the story of Panchali from the *Mahabharatha* in Tamil with a hidden motive, though he does not mention it anywhere. Panchali is the wife of the Pandavas (the good princes). Their leader looses everything in gambling and finally also his wife. She is now unprotected. As the enemies try to outrage her modesty and tear off her clothes, Krishna comes to her aid and extends the cloth miraculously. I think that Panchali stands for women in general and for India in particular. What Bharathi is saying is that we have not been protecting their honour and he is therefore shaming us into waking up and doing something.

Women would certainly be happy with this defence of Bharathi. The oppression of women continues in India. Female foetuses are selectively aborted. Female children are quietly done away with. As they grow up they are not treated equally with the male children. Wives are still persecuted for dowry and suicides and murders of such women are common. Financial independence through education and having a job enables women, especially among the middle classes, to defend themselves better in situations of oppression and to work for their liberation. Women today are no longer dependent on men to protect their rights. They can defend themselves and have become more ready to leave an oppressive marriage and to live alone if necessary.

An embodied mysticism

When I first read Bharathi's 'Song of Krishna' I had simply taken it as a collection of good devotional songs. I was intrigued with the idea of invoking Krishna not only as a male but also as a female. But later, when I was studying theology and reading Hindu devotional texts like Naradha's Bhakti Sutras, I understood that Bhakti exploits all possible human emotions and so imagines God in many different ways so as to love God in every possible way. Thus God can be looked at as Father and Mother, Lord and Servant, the Bridegroom and the Friend, the Son. I knew that in the *Nayaka-Nayaki bhava* (the Lord-Beloved manner), even in other religions, God was imagined as the male while the devotee became the female. So when I come back to Bharathi now I am still intrigued to see him imagining Krishna in female forms, not only as mother, but as bride. This is all the more surprising because the person so imagined is not simply God but an avatar of God who is male – an 'historical' figure. In imagining him as female one also flouts history.

Reading the songs again I am moved by their mystical depth. For all their varied human images, they are deeply apophatic. They sing of an Absolute beyond all name and form. So any name, or better image, whether male or female, really suits IT. Second, as opposed to an apophatic mysticism that denies every name, this affirms every name and image. But by affirming even contrary images like male and female it better transcends every image to reach the Absolute which goes beyond all images by including them. Third, by using multiple images every aspect of human emotion is involved. As a matter of fact, the poems show us that every dimension of human experience is evoked. So the loving relationship is rooted in the body and in society.

The Absolute is reached through symbols, but in that very activity the symbols are denied. In the Buddhist Mahayana tradition, there is a saying: 'Nirvana is *samsara*.' When you go beyond everything you rediscover everything in the Absolute. I think that Bharathi's experience of the Absolute is at this level. This is a very postmodern way of looking at symbol in language. But it leads, not to a chaotic pluralism, but to a deep apophatic convergence.

In an advaitic (non-dual) perspective, the Absolute can be seen not only in the images of others, but in actual humans. In the same way, nature also can be a mediation of the Absolute. So the Absolute appears in the form of nature. This is more clear when Bharathi sees the Absolute as Shakti. Today such a perspective may help an ecological outlook leading to respect for and protection of nature.

The film

A few years ago a film of Bharathi's life and message was made in Tamil. This also is a kind of re-reading. It is interesting that, while the national movement serves as a background for the story of his life, the focus is on his desire to free the people, especially the oppressed ones like Dalits and women. This supposes also freeing the others from their superstitious dependence on oppressive social structures. The film, however, highlights a dimension that we cannot see in the writings of Bharathi himself. It is the experience of poverty and social ostracism that he suffers because of his reformist views and zeal. The most painful experience is the inability of his own wife to share his ideals till the end. However, he comes across as a visionary who is not changed by his suffering, though he dies abandoned by society.

Conclusion

Bharathi is a great poet. He must have been an intense person, a mystic who saw his country and its people as images of God. His vision was holistic though he was aware of the dissonances like caste discrimination, oppression of women, colonial domination and exploitation of the poor. His quest is for freedom for every one and every thing. If he were alive today he would be sensitive to the desires of the downtrodden, whether they are Dalits, Tamils, women or nature. He would have respected cultural and religious pluralism and promoted harmony. His perspective would have been deeply religious: not a sectarian religion that divides, but a mysticism that unites. His advice to forgive one's enemies is indicative and rather rare in Hinduism.

> My heart, be graceful to your enemy!
> We see fire in the midst of smoke on this earth.
> Our Lord who is the form of love is present among our
>   enemies. (p. 213)

This certainly is advice that is very relevant to India today and to the world.

3

FOLLY TO THE RICH

Ernst Bloch's *Atheism in Christianity*

Roland Boer

A late-night train, a poor student reading and a man next to him who looks intently at the book's cover – this was the situation when I first read Ernst Bloch's *Atheism in Christianity* (1972). The bold, sans-serif letters across the front of the worn blue hardcover had attracted the eyes of my solitary neighbour on the train.

'Sorry to interrupt,' he said.

I looked up, blankly.

'I couldn't help noticing the title of the book you're reading.'

I said nothing.

'*Atheism in Christianity*? He went on. I've just become a Christian, so I want to find out more about what it means.'

This is not the book you want to read, I thought to myself. It'll help you, but not the way you expect. Instead, I said to him,

'It's a great book. One of the best I've read.'

He dug out a pen and a scrap of paper and wrote down the title. 'Why are you reading it?' he asked.

'Oh, I'm studying, um . . . divinity,' I replied.

'Divinity?'

'Yeah, theology . . . I said. Biblical studies, church history, theology – it's for a degree at Sydney Uni.'

'I didn't know you could study that at Sydney Uni, he went on. I'm thinking about going to Bible College to learn more about God.'

Divinity at Sydney Uni is not for you, I thought again.

'Why don't you check it out?' I said.

'I will,' he said. ' . . . Oh, here's my stop.' He stood up.

'Good luck,' I said.

'Thanks,' he replied. 'God bless.'

I didn't see him turn up for any classes, but that was no surprise and bit of a relief.

After he had gone, I re-entered Bloch's text, sinking into the words and sentences that did not quite make sense to me. Bloch was, if anything, enigmatic. Later I would realize it was his expressionistic style. What amazed me then, however, was the oxymoron he presented. Here was a German scholar who could write without anchoring his pages with weighty footnotes referring to every possible work written on the topic (and a few that weren't). That was a wonder to behold, and that alone was enough to keep me reading . . . as well as the craggy, stern face that glared at me from the back cover. Bloch was doing his best to look like a fire-breathing Hebrew prophet.

I was to learn much more about Bloch over the next two decades, so much so that his work became the focus of the long first chapter of the first tome, *Criticism of Heaven*, of my four-volume 'criticism' series. However, this is not another version of my CV (what some seem to regard as the epitome of so-called 'auto-biographical' narratives), where I become the bore at the bar who has had one too many drinks for the good of those around him.

Back then I was a skinny, chain-smoking student of theology at the University of Sydney. Sleeping too little, thinking too much of sex, drinking too much coffee with the consistency of tar, burning the midnight oil, blasting my ears with the music of Midnight Oil (or the Oils, as we called them), I was a candidate for the ministry in the Presbyterian Church of Australia – the Calvinist rump left over after most of the church united with the Methodists and Congregationalists in 1977. It was also before I had learned to be profoundly suspicious of auto-biographical stories, so I can give the impression of baring my soul – at least until the time when I did become much more suspicious of these sorts of things.

Now I don't smoke, I get up at dawn to write, drink tea,

blast my ears with (do I dare admit it?) Nick Cave and Jethro Tull, or still think a lot about sex. I am also no longer in the church. But then, these days, I am rather suspicious of these sorts of stories. So who can tell whether what I say now is fiction or not?

Back to Bloch at Sydney University in the mid-1980s. On the grass outside the library where I used to read, kangaroos grazed, we ate wombat stew for dinner, shoes were rare and books even rarer. We would tear them up and pass on the pages to one another when we had read them. At least, that's what my relatives in the Netherlands thought, as did many Europeans, who thought and still think of Australia as a rough frontier, full of Crocodile Dundees (the movie did come out about this time), Steve Irwins and potential princesses for randy European princes looking for a fertile woman to produce an heir to one or another throne – anything to breed out that lazy eye, floppy ear and lantern jaw. In fact, I have lost count of how many times someone, somewhere, has said that I look like Crocodile Dundee. From Taiwan to Tehran, from Groningen to Greenland, St Petersburg to St Louis-du-Ha-Ha! (the place does indeed exist, in Quebec), the same question has come time and again. Once, in a remote corner of Newfoundland, I was asked whether I was Paul Hogan's brother.

At Sydney University, I was taught by the energetic Barbara Thiering, the one with those crazy ideas about Qumran and the origins of the Jesus movement (she was able to retire on the handsome royalties from her book, *Jesus the Man*, which made it big with the New Age crowd and the myriad of disaffected church members). Perhaps because of such ideas, she turned out to be a great teacher, one who resolutely refused to foist her ideas on her students, and the one who first whetted my appetite for biblical studies and theology.

Ernst Bloch turned up in the midst of all this via the mild and soupy Jürgen Moltmann. In a course called 'Political and Liberation Theologies', taught to two of us (there were never more than two or three gathered . . .) by a grizzly 70-year-old Alan Loy, I had been reading Moltmann's *The Crucified God*. He mentioned Bloch a few times, especially the 'politics of hope', so instead of reading about him, I resolved to read the man himself. After all, who could resist a title like *Atheism in Christianity?*

This was a time when I became used to the idea that you read books by people who were no more than names and photographs – especially the 'big names'. The so-called cultural cringe was still very much part of Australian culture and academia: one looked overseas for the really serious work by the major figures. I'll never forget the shock of meeting such names in the flesh for the first time when I began travelling overseas. Again and again, I came face to face with that 'death of the author' experience, where the picture I had built up of one person or another did not quite match the reality. It first hit me when I actually listened to Moltmann, when he was in Montreal giving a series of lectures at McGill in the late 1980s. Here he was, talking, responding, smiling, and not merely a name with an aura. And he was not quite as impressive as I had been led to believe.

As for Bloch, who really was dead by the time I read him, I was able to figure out from his difficult texts the following: a) Bloch was a Marxist atheist; b) he was fascinated by the Bible; c) he argued that it has a revolutionary core that challenges all domination by the gods and earthly rulers. But he did so with these enigmatic sentences of which I struggled to make sense. They were breathless sentences, allusive, rushing on, as it were, to the Kingdom of God on earth (that is, communism).

At the time I was in full assault on the Calvinist heritage of my parents. Anything was useful ammunition – Roman Catholic monasticism, laziness, High Church rituals – but this was the best by far. A Marxist who claimed the Bible as a central text for the communists! Delicious. My parents had emigrated from the Netherlands in the late 1950s. As my maternal grandfather told me many years later when I asked him why they had emigrated en masse (they and their seven children – the clan now has 25 grandchildren and more than 30 great grandchildren), they wanted to find a place where there had been no world wars and where there was little chance of one. A look at the world map and Australia was about as far you could go.

My parents came from the breakaway *Gereformeerde Kerk* in the Netherlands, the conservative Calvinist wing that has become disillusioned by the creeping liberalism of the main Reformed Church of the Netherlands. The immigrants from the *Gereformeerde Kerk* established their own Reformed Church of Australia, of which my parents were members. So, with the Dutch I first spoke I also imbibed the deep assumptions and daily practices of Calvinism: prayer before all meals (even in public), a Bible reading after the evening meal, no study or watching television or going to the shops on Sunday. It always struck me as wonderfully strange that a tradition that stressed grace over the law could be so legalistic.

Eventually they had joined the Presbyterian Church precisely because it too had Calvinist roots (via the dour John Knox). So, in that grand tradition of the eldest son following in the footsteps of his ministerial father, I too studied theology for the sake of becoming a minister in the Church. By the time I took up theological study, I was working hard to distance myself as far as possible from the Calvinism of my childhood. Since the hard-line conservative Calvinists had recently won control of the Presbyterian Church, it was not long before I was at loggerheads with them as well. They would be the first who would kick me in the teeth so that eventually I would find much more pleasant pastures outside, although with a significant dentist's bill.

After reading Bloch on those train journeys, I had to find out more. Bloch was put aside. At the time, liberation theology was carrying on Bloch's legacy. It was still in full flower, maturing in its efforts to combine Marxist analysis of society with theological reflection. Yet, already there were the first murmurings of roping in these wayward liberationists, especially after one or two Roman Catholic priests had joined the guerrillas in Latin America. By this time, no one seriously looked for inspiration to the paradox of 'actually existing socialism' in Eastern Europe and the USSR, which was already unwinding under Gorbachev. Margaret Thatcher (infamous for her phrase, 'there is no such thing as society') and Ronald Reagan were reshaping the capitalist world in a re-packaged and vicious laissez-faire, The Rolling Stones (aka. The Strolling Bones) still seemed relatively youthful and Madonna had not yet worn her T-shirt, 'Kabbalists do it better'.

In this situation I read Marx and then Hegel, on that same daily train journey. Marx's *Capital* was my companion for many months, and then Hegel's difficult *Phenomenology of Spirit*. Yet, Bloch continued to haunt me as I wrote on Marx and Hegel. What would possess a Marxist – a hero (for a time) of the utopian effort at a new society in East Germany, at least until he fell foul of the powers that be when that effort ran aground, when minds closed and petty jealousies surfaced – to read the Bible so avidly?

By the end of the process of reading and writing on Marx and Hegel, I realized that this body of thought and political practice had a good deal going for it. Why, I wondered, did some of the best minds in the world find Marxism so intriguing and challenging, so much so that they sought to develop it further? I was never in their league, but I do remember thinking that if it was good enough for them, it was good enough for me. I was always just a little sceptical concerning the standard story of the rise of the West, of the advancement of the cause of freedom, democracy and Christianity, and here was a way of seeing history and our present that made it clear to me that we are far from such things.

This realization was not as sudden as that of my mother. Some years later I gave my father – who likes to make things – a selection of my own beer and a copy of *Novel Histories*. True to form, he later told me that he didn't like the beer and couldn't understand the book. Needless to say, I haven't offered him a beer since. But my mother read the book and then lay awake, unable to sleep and tormented by the blinding realization – 'Oh my God, my son is a Marxist! My son is a Marxist!'

My timing couldn't have been better. By the time I was convinced of the explanatory power of Marx in the late 1980s, the Berlin Wall was teetering and communism was soon to roll back in one peaceful revolution after another from Bulgaria to Lithuania. Euphoria gripped the capitalist West – 'we' had won the Cold War, thanks to that old hero of Z-grade Hollywood westerns who happened to be president of the USA. Euphoria gripped Eastern Europe as well, as people (they still tell me this story when I am there) believed they could step past capitalism and communism to a new future. Statues toppled, school history textbooks were rewritten (especially in the West), and maps were redrawn. Religious revival was sweeping the East, we were told, the shop shelves were full of items that no one could afford. The Church was back in business, and maybe even the heir to the Tsar would be back on the throne. Just as I had discovered Marx, everyone was saying, 'Karl who?' At least it became possible to pick up copies of Marx, Lenin and the rest of the bunch in second-hand bookshops which could hardy give them away fast enough. I was even given a gift of a bust of Lenin from a stall in Sofia, since no one wanted it there (he is a rather handsome fellow, with that chin of history pondering the coal ships from my study window).

During the 1990s, liberation theology slid out of sight, charismatic and Pentecostal missionaries made headway in Latin America as one government after another bowed to the wise recommendations of the International Monetary Fund and the World Bank, and George Bush Sr roughed up Saddam Hussein for his indiscretion of invading 'democratic' Kuwait. Everything looked rosy . . . At least until those planes bumped into the World Trade Center in New York on that day in September, 2001, and what turned out to be the Second Oil War got underway.

By the end of the 1990s, I returned to Bloch's *Atheism in Christianity*. In between my first and second reading, I had the misfortune to teach at a theological college in Sydney for some years. At one point in those long years, a student approached me:

'I've come to you since I know you are the most sceptical person here,' she said.

'That's a fair assessment,' I said, eyebrows raised.

'Would you tell me, then,' she said, 'do you believe in evil spirits?'

'Hmmm . . . ' I said.

She waited.

'Well, if you look closely,' I finally answered, 'you will see them follow me every time I walk in the front door. They sit on the roof corners, watch at the windows, and crouch behind the doorways waiting for some soul to possess. When I go, they follow me home.'

Go I finally did, although I made sure to wear sandals and dust them off as I walked out that door one last time. I also hoped it was the last time I had to go through an oedipal struggle. For a time I travelled weekly by bus from Sydney to Melbourne. A rather long trip to work, about 900km, it allowed plenty of time to read. By this time, I had managed to track down a copy of *Atheism in Christianity* of my own, from the same print run in 1972 by Herder and Herder, with the same blue cover and dust-jacket with a stern Herr Bloch on the back. The title now resonated with me in a new way, for I had started to feel that every time I walked in the door of that theological college to teach or go to one of the interminable meetings, I became an atheist. What is it, I wondered, about religion, especially Christianity, that can make one such an atheist? I had begun to think that it was a common outcome, and that those who stayed in the Church switched their belief to something else – especially the institution. One of them had indeed told me on more occasions than I care to remember, 'the show must go on'.

On that bus in the early days of the third millennium I read as much Bloch as possible, carefully, slowly, repeatedly. Usually they were night buses, and at times I read through most of the night, snuggled up against a plump Irish woman who kept offering me lollies, or against a neurotic chef who festooned his cloth travel-bag with padlocks, or against a jailbird (he was innocent!) who was on his way to see his children for the first time in five years, or against a 97-year-old man from Slovenia at whose place Slavoj Žižek played when he was a child, or against a former stripper from Tokyo who told me the story of the illness and death of her Persian cat, blow by harrowing blow, and then about the Doberman Pinschers of her old boy-friend (I made a mental note not to call).

Marxists, I thought, were not given to writing books about the Bible or theology. There are one or two, like Lucien Goldmann or Karl Kautsky or Theodor Adorno or Antonio Gramsci . . . well, actually quite a few, as I was still to learn, who have in fact written on the Bible and theology. But Bloch was the first and my introduction to this long tradition of some of the best minds in philosophy, literature and politics.

What Bloch says, it seems to me, is that the Bible is deeply multivalent on a political level. While it may not always be folly to the rich, it is also the Church's bad conscience. Bloch was puzzled and entranced by the fact that while the Bible taught all too often to serve your masters on earth and in heaven, it also stuck a huge finger at them at the same time. Sometimes he pushes things too far, when for example he argues that the earliest stratum of sources (he was writing during the heyday of German dominance in biblical historical criticism) reflected stories of rebellion and protest that were later edited into condemnations of those seditious stories. Or that there was a red thread that ran through from the serpent in the garden to the insurrections of Jesus of Nazareth, one that would eventually lead to the liberation of human beings from God. And guess where this teleology led him? To Marxist atheism, the final expression of the messianic tradition. Indeed, he seems to have been a bit of a jerk. Fixing people with his messianic stare, he was wont to rise at the close of a lecture or discussion and solemnly announce, 'truly the spirit has been with us today!' People couldn't help wondering whether he hadn't imbibed one or two spirits over breakfast.

For all his flaws (but that is part of what I like about him), Bloch also has an insight or two, such as his argument for political exegesis well before it became fashionable in biblical studies (but then biblical criticism always seems like the last kid on the block), or the idea of the discernment of myth, where one must discern between myths of rebellion over against those of oppression, or his (best) strategy: the argument that stories of insurrection survived not despite, but because of those stories of suppression. Why do we get so many stories of human rebellion that is crushed and punished? Why do human beings seem to sin against a stern God and brutal rulers, all rolled into one? From the murmuring in the wilderness against Moses to Vashti's condemnation in the book of Esther, there do seem to be an awful lot of these stories.

Here, it seemed to Bloch, lay the reason for the Bible's continued appeal to revolutionary groups. He carefully excavated the story of Thomas Müntzer, the firebrand reformer who took Luther's principles to their logical conclusion, became a revolutionary on the run until he finally lost his head (literally) leading an army of peasants with their pitchforks against the assembled heavy cavalry of the German princes. No points for guessing who won. Then there was Joachim of Fiore, with his theory of the three ages of the world, the final one of the spirit leading to the peaceable Kingdom. He might have added Gerrard Winstanley and the Diggers, who simply began cultivating common land, giving out the produce freely to anyone who would join them. The conservative thugs would have nothing of it and drove them out. Or the guerrilla priests at the revolutionary edge of liberation theology, who actually kept Bloch's work alive during its long neglect.

As the bus trips gradually added more distance between me and the stuffy feeling of the Church and its equally stuffy teaching institutions, Bloch brought me to a new position. I began to see that the easy option was to turn your back and walk out. Like me, so many have chosen to do so. But I began to admire those who took the much more difficult stand of staying inside, for whatever reason (that is beyond me), and struggling for the cause of women, gays and lesbians, people of colour, indigenous people, those impoverished, slaughtered and starving because of our economic system. God knows it is a futile struggle, for religious institutions are brutal, stuffy and conservative places. But I admire those who stay all the same, since it is the tough choice. Perhaps you can only see this from the outside.

I also realized that the strength and persuasiveness of Marxism lay not in its refusal of religion, especially Judaism and Christianity, but in its deep affinity with them. It was not for nothing that Bloch and his fellow travellers said so much about the Bible, theology, the Church and the Synagogue. It really is in the business of providing an alternative political myth that captures the imagination. As the much vaunted 'New World Order' (remember that slogan?) collapses all around us, with fear gripping one Western country after another, with an oil shock almost upon us, with the US hobbled in the Middle East, with countries putting together more and more pieces of police states, with the anti-capitalist movement inspiring a generation of teenagers, it seems that Left thought and practice is back, although in ways that the old warhorses of the Left hardly expected.

Finally, it seemed to me that Max Weber had pinpointed only one element of Calvinism. As most of you will know, Weber famously argued that Protestantism, especially in its Calvinist form, paved the way for capitalism. By breaking up the monasteries, it turned asceticism, discipline and denial into a daily practice of work. It taught frugality and dependence on God's grace, as well as obedience to the powers that be. Once it had done its task, it could quietly disappear, or in Weber's phrase, it was a vanishing mediator. In his opposition to Marx – setting out to show how beliefs and ideas were more powerful than mere material factors such as the economy – he also missed something. And that was the way Calvinism also was a forerunner of Marxism. Some of its crucial ideas fed into Marxism, such as predestination (crudely the infamous claim that 'history is on our side'; more subtly the realization that what looks like freedom of choice is nothing of the sort) and grace (revolutions always break out from entirely unexpected quarters; they are entirely undeserved). Needless to say, I have made my peace with Calvin.

Perhaps it's time to take Bloch with me again, as a companion on my long-awaited journeys by tramp steamer. Who knows who will stop by my chair as I sit, book open, on the deck among the containers? Will it be one of the sailors who has just danced with a fellow sailor at the crossing of the equator? Will it be an engineer who is thinking about studying theology? Will it be someone who asks me whether I believe in mermaids? Or perhaps a militant from *Sea Shepherd*, on her way to join her protest ship?

Reference

Ernst Bloch (1972), *Atheism in Christianity*, New York: Herder & Herder.

4

NATHAN A. SCOTT JR.'S
THE WILD PRAYER OF
LONGING

David Jasper

In 1975, I was nearing the end of studying for a degree in theology at the University of Oxford, and half way through my training for ordination in the Church of England. My seminary, St Stephen's House, was High Anglican and exuded a general smugness and intellectual conservatism that would have been unbearable had it not been for the presence in Oxford of such marvellous people as Maurice Wiles, the Regius Professor of Theology, Peter Baelz, the Regius Professor of Moral Theology, Peter Bide, the Chaplain at Lady Margaret Hall, and Dennis Nineham, the Warden of Keble College, where I was later to embark on a happy time of research in nineteenth-century literature and theology under the tutelage of Geoffrey Rowell, now the Anglican Bishop in Europe. For one reason or another, I was fortunate enough to have personal links with all of these people in the early stages of my theological reflections, and I also appreciated (and continue to value) the insistence in the Oxford course of study on reasonable skills in New Testament Greek, a solid grounding in the Church Fathers, and a decent overall knowledge of the Bible, church history and systematic theology. And yet I was deeply unhappy, not (as I think I would be now) because there was the insistence that theology was only and exclusively Christian, but because I was quite unable to connect the study of theology with the imaginative demands and critical disciplines of my first academic love, which was English literature, and which I had studied first as an undergraduate in Cambridge in the late 1960s, largely under the benign eye of Raymond Williams.

Then, one day, and quite by accident, I came across a book in Blackwell's bookshop by an American author I then had not heard of, and it was, quite simply, the title that caught my eye and drew my attention: it was Nathan A. Scott Jr.'s *The Wild Prayer of Longing: Poetry and the Sacred*. This slim volume was dedicated to one of my favourite North American novelists, Ralph Ellison, author of that wonderful book *Invisible Man*, 'with enduring affection', and yet there it was, not in Literature but in the Theology section. Even as I read the Preface, Scott's book began to articulate two things that were already dimly present in my mind. The first, more than a little disturbing for a young ordinand who was expecting to be making a living within the ministry of the Church, was a sense that the theology to which I was devoting myself (and quite possibly its practical application) was already largely culturally isolated and set apart from the wider study of the humanities. Scott says it in his first sentence: 'The new theologians of the present time, whatever their affiliation (Roman, Anglican, or Protestant), have of late been nervously remarking a profound erosion of the theological terrain as the chief religious fact of our period' (p. 1). This is familiar enough now, but it was not then, over thirty years ago. The second thing was, for me, closely related to the first. It was the sense that much of the language and vocabulary that I was learning to use in theology actually took on a much more authentic meaning and significance not in the Church but in the rather different context of literature and poetry. Scott said it precisely:

> And the contemporary cultural scene is replete with evidences which suggest that one of the principal issues of our age concerns the possibility of the modern imagination finding its ballast in a sacramental realism which is independent of the supernaturalist projections of traditional piety. (p. xiii)

It was simply a fact that in my life as a theological student I was being drenched each day in liturgical expressions of 'traditional piety', and yet it was in the continued reading of the poets, now devoured in my spare time rather in the manner of the guilty child who reads by torchlight under the bedclothes when the lights have been switched off, that I sensed something of what Scott called 'sacramental realism'. And it was a remarkable coincidence that the one poet to whom I was peculiarly addicted at the time, Theodore Roethke, was the subject of the last chapter of *The Wild Prayer of Longing*.

It all seemed too good to be true. I cannot recall sharing my find with anyone else at the time. It was more than a decade before Terry Eagleton was to write his *Literary Theory: An Introduction* (1983), but I had been at least aware of Terry as a postgraduate student of Williams at Jesus College, Cambridge when I had been an undergraduate there. And a quotation from an early Professor of English Literature at Oxford in the first part of the twentieth century was to jump off the page of Eagleton's book, and I suppose, in its stilted and rather pompous way, it reflected a sense driven deep into me long before in the English Faculty in the Cambridge of F. R. Leavis and then of Williams that it might, in a sense, hold a truth:

> England is sick, and . . . English literature must save it. The Churches (as I understand) having failed, and social remedies being slow, English literature now has a triple function: still, I suppose, to delight and instruct us, but also, and above all, to save our souls and heal the State. (Eagleton 1996, p. 20)

So, even while I was immersed in Oxford theology, and training for the Anglican priesthood, there was a sense that literature continued to mean more to me than the intellectual and perhaps spiritual stuff of the clerical profession, and Scott, for the first time, seemed to offer me a new way in the study that was to become my lifelong work and passion: the study of literature *and* theology – seen as a creative unit.

This in no way involved an abandonment of theology and its, to me, then and even now, somewhat odd subsection known as biblical studies, which I have always regarded as a rather eccentric bye-way of literary criticism, though, of course, the latter actually has its origins very largely, if not exclusively, in biblical hermeneutics. (This is a truth not generally acknowledged in departments of English literature.) Instead Scott's book allowed the language and narratives of Christian theology actually to come to life and be tested in the strategies and experience of literature. I had a deep suspicion back in the 1970s, surely with the arrogance of youth but I think a grain of truth, that most theologians, and the majority of the clergy whose ranks I was shortly to join, did not have a particularly sophisticated understanding of literature and were often not especially well read. Still, and against this observation, before I return to a more detailed review of Scott's book, I need to record that this chance literary encounter brought me into touch with a group of people, theologians and some Anglican parsons, most though not all of them in Oxford, whose wisdom and friendship were in future years to have the most profound effect on me. First and above all there was Dr F. W. Dillistone, Chaplain of Oriel College and former Dean of Liverpool Cathedral, one of the most gentle and wisest of souls, who led the way in Great Britain in the study of literature and theology. There was Fr Martin Jarrett-Kerr CR, an Anglican monk and a friend of Nathan Scott, and Dr John Coulson of Bristol University, whose book *Religion and Imagination* (1981) was largely responsible for my own initial research in nineteenth-century literature. And finally, Professor Elisabeth Jay, now of Oxford Brookes University, who was then, like myself, at the very beginning of an academic career, and similarly finding her way through the riches of often forgotten pathways of Victorian literature and religion.

And how is all this related to my first reading of *The Wild Prayer of Longing*? Well, from the very beginning of the book, Nathan picks up the two writers in the nineteenth century who had already begun to fascinate me above all others: on the first page there is a reference to Friedrich Nietzsche and his allusion to the death of God in *The Gay Science*, an 'event' which has haunted me ever since, not least through the work of, and later my friendship with, Tom Altizer, a radical American theologian to whom Scott refers in his book, though not by name. Then on page 2 is mentioned another Friedrich – Schleiermacher – who attracted me not so much as a theologian but as the 'father of modern hermeneutics' and through his theory of interpretation which provides the link between theological reflection and literary criticism and theory. Then, even as I read Scott's Preface, still standing in the second-hand section of Blackwells, page after page provided links to writers or themes that were central to my own thinking and interests, but which had not been remotely touched upon in my introductory theological studies in the Oxford Schools. The exception to this was Nathan's reference to the issue of liturgical language and above all the language of the Anglican Book of Common Prayer and its relation to the 'sacramental question . . . as to what it is in the nature of reality that can be counted on finally to sanctify human existence' (Scott 1971, xiv). Already I had lived for years at home aware of liturgical renewal and liturgical language through my father, a liturgist and the Chairman of the Church of England Liturgical Commission as it worked on what was to become The Alternative Service Book of 1980. Also, one of my teachers in Cambridge, Professor David Frost, was a member of the Commission, and he had the habit of trying out on his students the language of new collects or his new translation of the Psalms as exercises in 'practical criticism'. But then, and more excitingly for me, there was the reference to Erich Auerbach, whose famous chapter in *Mimesis* (1946) entitled 'Odysseus' Scar', comparing a passage in Homer's *Odyssey* with Genesis 22 (the Sacrifice of Isaac), I had tried out on a totally uncomprehending Old Testament tutor who could not see what this had to do with proper 'Old Testament scholarship'. There was also a footnote to Theodore Roszak's *The Making of a Counter Culture: Reflections on the Technocratic Society and its Youthful Opposition* (1969), a book which I had devoured in my last year in Cambridge. That had brought William Blake into a new perspective (later to be linked with the thought of the aforementioned Tom Altizer in a radical rethinking of what I understood as Christology), and introduced me to Norman Brown, Alan Ginsberg and Herbert Marcuse. It is one of those now dated books which I still have on my shelves, unread for years but redolent of a particular ethos and moment of intellectual and spiritual evolution, staring back at me like an old photograph of familiar faces that are barely recognizable from their long hair, large glasses and touching youthful optimism. There were also, in Scott's Preface, the poets Wallace Stevens and Robert Lowell and finally a reference to 'the immensely fruitful ideas of Martin Heidegger' (p. 2) of whose forbidding work *Being and Time* I had begun to realize the importance (though little of the sense) in the then quite new translation of an admired Oxford professor – John Macquarrie.

All this was just in the Preface. In half an hour, still standing in the bookshop, I had begun in a very preliminary way to piece together how I might now want to do theology as it might be meaningful for me. At the heart of *The Wild Prayer of Longing* is what Scott calls the 'sacramental vision', a term which enfleshed for me the modus vivendi into which I was being formed at an Anglican theological college in the High Church tradition with its daily Eucharist and Offices. It has remained with me ever since, though in Scott it was without the preciosity tinged with arrogance that seemed to go with it in High Anglicanism, and incorporated simultaneously both the stuff of the literature which made sense to me and the critical, counter-cultural ethos that allowed one to be simultaneously radical and traditional, tentative and committed.

Then, later on in my room, it was reading the final chapter, 'The Example of Roethke', which brought it all together. I admit now that I have not read Roethke for years, at least until I began to think about this chapter, but I realize as I look at my tattered, heavily annotated copy of the *Collected Poems*, bought in 1968, that I must have been at one point absorbing its 'wild disordered language of the natural heart' almost daily alongside my dutiful study of biblical commentaries, Karl Barth and what was to me then (though not now) the rather artificial theology of the Church Fathers. What I realize now is that it was precisely that combination of literature and theology that was so important, and I am grateful that Oxford expected at least a decent competence in the biblical languages and a sense of the arc of theological thinking from Athanasius and Augustine to scholasticism, the theology of the Reformation, through to Higher Criticism and German theology of the last two hundred years. But it was Scott's luminous prose that brought it alive, with its precise cadences, its locating of theological terms in 'the poetic universe of our period' and its celebration of aesthetics and the imagination in seemingly every corner of the literary universe. Scott begins his study of Roethke with a reference to Philip Wheelwright's seminal book of 1954, *The Burning Fountain* and its fourfold way of regarding the imagination within 'the world's multifarious reality', a passing comment on Heidegger and, by implication, Rudolf Otto's *The Idea of the Holy* (1917). The scene having been set, the chapter follows close critical readings of Roethke's poetry as profound theological expressions of experience from the gladsome to the despairing. Here I was in my element, and could begin to use the religious terminology I was beginning to acquire as a tool in the literary criticism of the poems such that at one and the same time I began to understand the poetry more clearly, and also theology began to be 'real' in a way I had never before known. Martin Buber, Conrad Bonifazi (whose 1967 book *A Theology of Things* I had encountered and thought better of than its sad neglect might suggest), then Emerson and Carl Jung interweave in Scott's discourse with the themes of literary criticism from the late New Critical period with which I was familiar – the intentional fallacy, close reading, a concern for semantics, and so on. Looking back now it does seem somewhat lush and even occasionally self-indulgent, but then it spoke directly to my youthful and distinctly a-historical romanticism which was labouring over the rather desiccated pages of historical-critical biblical critics and would eventually cut its research teeth in a doctoral study of Samuel Taylor Coleridge (pursued, incidentally, in a theology department and examined by none other than Don Cupitt!).

And so what of *The Wild Prayer of Longing* now, re-read after a period of 31 years since that day in Blackwells bookshop? First, it is read today through the lens of a long, not always easy, friendship with Nathan, who died in 2006, which allowed me to collect not only many of his books, both earlier and later than *The Wild Prayer*, but also signed copies of numerous articles in different journals as well as one or two treasured typescripts of writings that I believe were never published. These include essays on film and religion, a study which he took with the utmost seriousness even as early as the 1940s, long before the current crop of not always distinguished books in that field. They trace a mind sensitive to the work of lesser known contemporary poets as well as engaging in solid studies of George Orwell, on the one hand, and Paul Tillich on the other. One of his last authored books, *The Poetics of Belief* (1985), contains learned essays on Coleridge, Mathew Arnold and Walter Pater, and encouraged me to contribute my own thoughts on Pater as a chapter in Nathan's Festschrift volume, *Morphologies of Faith* (1990). There is a 1990 essay entitled 'Steiner on Interpretation' in the University of Notre Dame journal *Religion and Literature* which was a kind of prelude to Scott's last major publication, a volume of essays by a number of scholars (co-edited with Ronald A. Sharp) on the work of Georg Steiner, a polymath with whom Scott shares many characteristics. As I review this collection before me on my desk, I become aware of my own simultaneous closeness to and distance from Nathan, a distance that I think finally disappointed and even somewhat perplexed him in the latter years of our friendship. For if Nathan entered college in the early 1940s from a background utterly different from my own, I began university in the late 1960s and by the mid-1970s was ready to encounter the new world of literary theory in Paul de Man and many others, and also deconstruction in another book which I devoured almost as soon as it appeared in English in 1976, Jacques Derrida's *Of Grammatology*. This was a world that Scott could not abide, and perhaps did not always understand. His background in the 40s and 50s led him to different preoccupations, theologically rooted in Reinhold Niebuhr and Paul Tillich, while mine was in the counter-culture of the 60s, and I was happy to be allowed to take things apart in a theological journey which has taken me eventually into more apophatic regions of the spirit, less conscious, I suppose, of the poetry of civic virtue (the title of one of Nathan's books on Eliot, Malraux and Auden, published in 1976). We parted company finally, I think, though we continued to correspond, during a visit I made to the University of Virginia in the mid-1980s when I lectured with an unwitting lack of tact towards

Scott, on the theology of one of his colleagues at that university, Robert P. Scharlemann who had also written a book on Paul Tillich, but one stressing the theme of doubt as a methodological procedure in theology, and whose emphasis on negativity was alien to Scott's whole frame of reference.

But returning to *The Wild Prayer of Longing*, I can now appreciate why his work remains important and why I hope it is not forgotten as the next generation of students and scholars in the field of theology and literature begin their work through the filter of their own experience and intellectual and spiritual histories. First, Scott is a wonderful writer. In an age when academics are being forced more and more into scribbling for the ever increasing managerial and financially driven systems of the academy, producing work which is rarely attractive or of literary merit in itself, Nathan stands out as a scholar who has given both time and attention to the way in which he writes so that his prose combines complexity with utter lucidity, a medium which allows perfectly finessed thinking to be sustained by an English style that is capable of conveying its message not only by what it says but in the way that it says it. Here, for example, is his summary of Theodore Roethke 'definition of sanctity':

> . . . plotting for more than oneself, for the care of the good earth, in order that things might simply be what their entelechies intend that they shall be. (p. 94)

Second, obvious in this sentence is his overwhelming sense of responsibility as a scholar. Terry Eagleton once described nicely the tendency of the post-structuralists of my generation that we cheerfully adopted strategies of reading that too often allowed us 'to drive a coach and horses through everybody else's beliefs while not saddling you with the inconvenience of having to adopt any yourself'. There was indeed a degree of irresponsibility in the literary (and later theological) fashions of the 1980s such that by the end of the decade and into early years of the next books were appearing like J. Hillis Miller's *The Ethics of Reading* (1987) or Simon Critchley's *The Ethics of Deconstruction* (1992, revised edn 2005) which sought to rescue Derrida and others from the suggestion that they offered merely a kind of nihilistic freedom that lay outside the realm of values or even morals. Now, while it is certainly more complicated than that, the point is a valid one and perhaps especially those of us who remained in the field of theological studies were aware of the need to give new attention to ethical and moral issues in a postmodern age across the horizons of the religious, the political and the social. At this point Scott's fierce adhesion to the public sphere remains a continuing timely reminder. It is noteworthy that the last major work of Nathan's natural successor as a leader in the field of religion and literature studies in the United States, Robert Detweiler, a slightly younger scholar who is deeply immersed in the postmodern turn in religious thinking, was entitled *Uncivil Rites: American Fiction, Religion and the Public Sphere* (1996). Nor should we in Europe think that we are exempt from such anxieties regarding the civic realm.

My third point of commendation seeking to restore Nathan Scott to the new and the next generation of readers is, I suppose, at once both a strength and a weakness. I have made the obvious point that he and I could hardly have come from more different backgrounds. He an African American born in Cleveland and brought up in Detroit, me a son of a Church of England vicarage with a boyhood lived against the background of an English cathedral, south London and later Westminster. But what we have in common is ordination into the Anglican Communion with its deep and broad sense of tradition and liturgical practice. Although that is now perhaps terminally on the wane, I suspect I am still of a generation, and it is possibly the last, which is embraced by that capaciousness that allows the critical spirit to exist alongside the will to believe in a peculiar degree and has traditionally allowed the voice of the poet to be heard through the prose of theology, and freedom of interpretation to be exercised within wide parameters of doctrinal statement. In this sense it is not unreasonable to place Scott in the great tradition of Richard Hooker, Bishop Butler and John Keble, clergymen of the Church of England whose writings are as fine as literature as they are learned and wise as theology. Certainly I cannot follow them even at a remote distance, but

I can recognize the tenor of the voice, and perhaps it was this echo that I heard that day in the Oxford bookshop in 1975.

Now, what Nathan certainly lacked is something that we have rightly had brought to our attention as scholars of religion, and it is what might be called the spirit of global sensitivity. My theological training in the 1970s never once mentioned traditions other than the Christian, even in biblical studies. Over the years, in one way or another, I have stumbled my way into the riches of Jewish thought, into Islam and the great religions of the East. Now the study of theology has also been transformed by varieties of feminist critique, postcolonial studies and beyond, new voices from around the world, and certainly the students of my university in Glasgow are today much better qualified in these broad reaches of theology and religious studies than I ever was, and I am glad of it. But there is little or nothing of this in any of Scott's work.

And yet the study of literature and theology that he pursued does persist in new ways, both more and less well informed, in universities and colleges and not only in North America and the United Kingdom but worldwide, though largely at the postgraduate level. It is probably right that it has not become entirely institutionalized, existing on the borders in a variety of ways. (A volume published in 1983 to which Nathan Scott contributed, and edited by Robert Detweiler, was entitled *Art/Literature/Religion: Life on the Borders*.) It exists between the formal categories set by the academy, and yet in a process of continual renewal it remains a creative way of 'doing theology' and studying literature. In each new generation of students there are some who recognize its liberating possibilities and its challenges, finding teachers who have managed to cope with the limitations of their institutions, working in a genuinely interdisciplinary and ever renewed way which is often against the grain of the formal structures and funding systems which generate the frequently heard but vacuous rhetoric of 'interdisciplinarity'. Nathan A. Scott Jr. was a pathfinder in his own time in this study of literature and theology and genuinely interdisciplinary. He did not found a school of thought, nor a department at the University of Virginia which could be passed on to later generations. He was a highly competent and professional academic who at the same time had to find his own language between disciplines, a language which was at once efficient and also poetic and prophetic. Re-reading *The Wild Prayer of Longing* one is reminded of how many themes in that book anticipate contemporary theological discussions: for example, in chapter 2, Scott looks back to Harvey Cox's *The Secular City* (1965), but also forward to the work today of scholars like Graham Ward and others in their concern with the metropolis and the modern city. And yet he was a one-off, and perhaps that is why I found him so inspiring and fruitful for me in 1975. For he spoke in critical languages which I could understand, but in a new way, thereby encouraging me to try it for myself and in my own way. That is something I have continued to try and do, ever more convinced that the work of literature and theology must have an element of its own creativity, not only in its thinking but in its forms of writing. Thus, although Nathan Scott's work has, undoubtedly, dated, it has a certain timeless quality that shows us who follow him not so much what to do as how to do it, and to do it with learning and flair – and perhaps a certain amount of arrogance, balancing, as his colleague Anthony C. Yu once wrote, 'with enormous intelligence, skill, and erudition the claims and counterclaims of two venerable disciplines' (Yu 1990, p. xii).

References

E. Auerbach (1946, new impression 1969), *Mimesis: The Representation of Reality in Western Literature*, New Haven: Princeton University Press.

J. Coulson (1981), *Religion and Imagination: In Aid of a Grammar of Assent*, Oxford: Oxford University Press.

H. Cox (1965), *The Secular City: A Celebration of its Liberties and an Invitation to its Discipline*, New York: Macmillan.

S. Critchley (1992, rev. edn 2005), *The Ethics of Deconstruction: Levinas and Derrida*, New Dehli: Motilal Banarsidass.

R. Detweiler (ed.) (1983), *Art/Literature/Religion: Life on the Borders*, Atlanta: Scholars' Press.

R. Detweiler (1996), *Uncivil Rights: American Fiction, Religion, and the Public Sphere*, Urbana: University of Illinois Press.

T. Eagleton (1996), *Literary Theory: An Introduction*, 2nd edn, Oxford: Blackwell.

J. H. Miller (1987), *The Ethics of Reading: Kant, de Man, Eliot, Trollope, James*, New York: Columbia University Press.

T. Roethke (1966), *Collected Poems*, New York: Doubleday.

T. Roszak (1969), *The Making of a Counter Culture: Reflections on the Technocratic Society and Its Youthful Opposition*, New York: Doubleday.

N. A. Scott Jr. (1971), *The Wild Prayer of Longing: Poetry and the Sacred*, New Haven: Yale University Press.

N. A. Scott Jr. (1985), *The Poetics of Belief: Studies in Coleridge, Arnold, Pater, Santayana, Stevens and Heidegger*, Durham: University of North Carolina Press.

A. C. Yu (1990), 'Nathan A. Scott, Jr., An Appreciation', in Mary Gerhart and Anthony C. Yu, *Metaphors of Faith: Essays in Religion and Culture in Honor of Nathan A. Scott, Jr.*, Atlanta: Scholars Press, 1990.

5

'TO SEE THE GREAT DECEIT WHICH IN THE WORLD DOTH LIE'

Christopher Hill's *The World Turned Upside Down*

Christopher Rowland

The circumstances surrounding my initial acquaintance and first reading of Christopher Hill's *The World Turned Upside Down: Radical Ideas During the English Revolution* are themselves strange and reflect the contraries of both the book's content, its author and the situation in which I read it. I was at once enthralled by the extraordinary people who wrote the writings described in the book.

Peter Nolan (now Sinyi Professor of Chinese Management at the Judge Business School, at Cambridge University) and I became fellows of Jesus College, where he remains, on the same day in 1979. He had just been appointed to be an assistant lecturer in economics, and I, to be Dean of Jesus College. Peter, it would be fair to say, didn't have much time for Christianity. The dinner following the admission of fellows is a disorientating occasion by any standards, but it was the context in which we had an animated conversation about Christianity and my political and radical sympathies. Peter was surprised that I not only knew about, but also sympathized with, a Marxist critique of religion. In that context he asked me if I had read Christopher Hill's book. I had not. The incongruity of discovering about seventeenth-century radicals in the rarefied atmosphere of a Cambridge college has never entirely been lost on me. But it is a paradox which has continued to puzzle and amuse. For one thing, Hill, Marxist that he was, managed to combine his convictions with being a much-loved Master of an Oxford college. In one sense, both Hill and I could be accused of armchair radicalism, but as I read and explored the writings which are discussed in this book, it soon became clear (and this was confirmed by Hill's later writings) that these ideas too had a history. It was not the case of a short outburst of radicalism which burnt brightly then just fizzled out. At the end of the seventeenth century, the radicals too had to come with 'the experience of defeat' (to use the title of another Christopher Hill book). Some didn't abandon their convictions but explored ways of maintaining them in the unpromising situation of a greater demand for social conformity. That struggle, which I saw in the writings of Milton and, indeed, in what might have become of Gerrard Winstanley, represented the ongoing problem for all those with radical political convictions who had to live in very changed political situations. This was very much a live issue for me, as 1979 marked the beginning of the Thatcher era. It was in my view the late twentieth-century equivalent of the restoration of Church and monarchy in the middle of the seventeenth century.

Indeed, there was a clear relationship between how it was that the college which employed me saw itself and that event, so disastrous for the radicals. Annually, there was a service of Commemoration of Benefactors in which there was a corporate narrative in which 'the happy restoration of Church and monarchy' in the seventeenth century was applauded. The problem for me was that I as Dean was required to read this out. I compromised by omitting the epithet 'happy', so that the narrative read solely as a description rather than a value judgement! I salved my conscience by thinking that the compromises, which Winstanley, Milton and others had to make, were far more demanding of them than this was of me.

It is difficult to overestimate the impact that reading *The*

World Turned Upside Down had on me, both intellectually and existentially. I was thereby introduced to the seventeenth-century religion of England, its vibrancy, militancy, creativity and enthusiasm. As with many others whose training had been done in traditional theological faculties, there was a gap in my knowledge of the early modern period (still replicated in my own university). It is incredible that the age of Locke and Hobbes and Milton, Donne and Marvell, not to mention the amazing writers who figure in Hill's book, remain beyond the pale of many theology and religious studies syllabuses. Existentially it was, if anything, more important. As I eagerly devoured the book in a weekend, I found that I was reading about people whose theological views I shared. Like many others, my fascination was then, and still is, with the extraordinary writing career of Gerrard Winstanley. It only lasted four years, and we know so little about his early life, and, more particularly, what became of him after he shot to fame in the immediate aftermath of the execution of Charles I in 1649. If I concentrate on Winstanley in this chapter, that is because he has been a catalyst for so much of my thinking about theology and contemporary practice in the thirty years since I discovered him through Hill's book. It is Winstanley whose work lies in large part behind my attempt in 1988 to outline what we mean by radical Christianity (*Radical Christianity: A Reading of Recovery*), in the collection I edited with Andrew Bradstock in 2002 (*Radical Christian Writers: A Reader*), and, most recently, in my quest to understand the biblical hermeneutics of William Blake.

In Winstanley's extant writing there is such a remarkable conjunction of theology and practice: 'action is the life of all' is something of a catchphrase, which is taken from a remarkable passage of an autobiography by Winstanley:

> Not a full year since, being quiet at my work, my heart was filled with sweet thoughts, and many things were revealed to me which I never read in books, nor heard from the mouth of any flesh, and when I began to speak of them, some people could not bear my words, and amongst those revelations this was one, That the earth shall be made a common Treasury of

livelihood to whole mankind, without respect of persons; and I had a voice within me bad me declare it all abroad, which I did obey, for I declared it by word of mouth to whosesoever I came, then I was made to write a little book called, The New Law of Righteousnesse, and therein I declared it; yet my mind was not at rest, because nothing was acted, and thoughts run in me, that words and writings were all nothing, and must die, for action is the life of all, and if thou dost not act, thou dost nothing. Within a little time I was made obedient to the word in that particular likewise; for I took my spade and went and broke the ground upon George-hill in Surrey, thereby declaring freedom to the Creation, and that the earth must be set free from entanglements of Lords and Landlords, and that it shall become a common Treasury to all, as it was first made and given to the sons of men (A Watch-Word to the City of London and the Army – August 1649).

Radicalism has always been part of the fabric of Christian theology and life. Throughout Christian history, there have been writings that have criticized political arrangements, promoted change, and, most important of all, have advocated active engagement for change, rather than merely writing about it. A characteristic of many of the texts in Hill's book is the strong sense of vocation of the writers, who believed that they were called to challenge received wisdom and practice. Theirs is not the abstract reflection of theologians, but theology forged in the midst of active engagement with the injustices and sufferings of the people of the world. They were convinced that God was calling them, like the prophets and apostles before them (cf. Galatians 1.1) to engage in what they were doing.

Reading *The World Turned Upside Down* and deeper immersion in liberation theology, both as a result of direct exposure to it in Brazil and also grassroots movements in Britain, led me to explore radical Christianity. I discovered many common ingredients, including a critique of false religion, a hope for a new world, but one that is to be found on earth and not in heaven. Eschatological hope was not a matter of speculation but realization, as it was for the first Christians and with which the New Testament is replete. The coming reign of God is believed to be in some sense already present. So, the Present becomes the Decisive Moment in the Divine Purposes, called in the New Testament a *Kairos* (Mark 1.15). It is a time of crisis and a moment of opportunity. This opportunity relativizes all previous relationships and hierarchies, and there is an intimate interaction between the human and the divine as the Divine Spirit, poured out on all flesh, is at work, revolutionizing relationships, attitudes to wealth, knowledge and power relations.

As a biblical scholar, what particularly fascinated me about the seventeenth-century writings (and has continued to do so as I have extended my in-depth study to include the work of writers like William Blake) is the use of the Bible. Preoccupation with the literal sense of the text has become a dominant feature of post-Reformation hermeneutics (and in many ways has been supported by historical-critical study of the Bible). What matters is the meaning of the text 'in and for itself', rather than what it may mean for the reader. That is the direct antithesis of the readings of the seventeenth-century radicals, as it is of the liberation theologians and the grassroots communities which inspire them. Here we find a rejection of the priority of the written text of scripture and a subordination of it to the inner understanding which comes through the Spirit. It is an engagement with the Bible which is not cut off from the existential commitments and concerns of the interpreters. The scriptures, therefore, become the catalyst for discernment of the divine way in the present. What counts is not so much what the text meant, but what import these words may have in the circumstances of the present. Action and commitment are the context of knowledge of the divine will.

Our knowledge of Gerrard Winstanley is very sketchy, apart, that is, from the remarkable experiment in digging the common land in Surrey weeks after the execution of Charles I. He writes of the present as a moment when the reordering of society in line with God's purpose is now imminent (Sabine 1941: 170, cf. 153, 184, 410). From April 1649 to March 1650 Winstanley's career and writing were intimately bound up with the Digger commune set up in Surrey. As the term 'Digger' implies, the group of which Winstanley was a member were concerned to give practical effect to their convictions. He was prompted by a revelation that he and his companions should dig the common land, thus claiming what they regarded as their rightful inheritance (*True Levellers Standard*, Sabine 1941: 260–2). Winstanley and a few others moved to St George's Hill, Cobham, on 1 April 1649, and their number grew to about forty (there appear to have been similar experiments taking place at roughly the same time). Their action provoked hostility from local landowners and complaints to the Council of State. They were finally driven off the land in the spring of 1650. We know little of Winstanley's background except that he originated in Wigan, and even less of what became of him. The burst of writing is confined to a period of less than five years. His last extant writing is a despairing and tragic lament about the apparent failure of his hopes. He writes of seeing 'the great deceit which in the world doth lie: men saying one thing now, unsaying it anon, breaking all's engagements, when deeds for him are done' (*Law of Freedom in a Platform*, Sabine 1941: 600).

Fundamental to the communal experiment of the Diggers was the belief that the earth was a common treasury, and, as such, the whole concept of the ownership of land as private property conflicted with this fundamental right. Winstanley was concerned to expose the way in which the elevation of private property to a universal human good reflected a fundamental characteristic of humanity after the Fall of Adam. Private property, he argued, was the curse of Adam, and those who possess it have gained it by oppression, murder or theft. The rule of the Serpent manifests itself in four ways: a professional ministry; the kingly power; the judiciary and the buying and selling of the earth.

Winstanley's understanding of the struggle within the individual, and in society at large, is pervaded with the apocalyptic imagery of the book of Revelation. This is seen in his early tract, 'The Breaking of the Day of God', which is an extended commentary on the two witnesses of Revelation 11, a subject of intense debate in the history of interpretation of that chapter (Kovacs and Rowland 2004: 126–30). Winstanley suggests that the two witnesses are Jesus and the Saints, so that down the centuries the whole history of 'witness' against the power of the Beast is all part of the same task of 'bruising the serpent's head'. Such witnesses are those who 'can prove their testimony not from books but from their own experienced knowledge' (Sabine 1941: 88). The struggle between good and evil, therefore, is viewed through the lens of that between the Dragon and Christ (cf. Rev. 12). It is now linked to the advocacy of a true commonwealth, in which one will not lord it over another. Spiritual regeneration and structural change are intimately linked: when the earth becomes a common treasury, as it was in the beginning, and 'the King of Righteousness comes to rule in every one's heart, then he kills the first Adam' ('Fire', Sabine 1941: 468–70; Hill 1973: 268). This was not in some remote future but was an imminent and this-worldly fulfilment. The new heaven and earth is something to be seen here and now, therefore, for royal power is the old heaven and earth that must pass away. Christ's second coming was the establishment of a state of community in the present, for it is 'the fullness of time' ('True Levellers Standard', Sabine 1941: 61 cf. 184; Hill 1973: 86–7). God is not located far above the heavens, therefore, but is to be found in the lives and experiences of ordinary men and women. The perfect society will come when there takes place 'the rising up of Christ in sons and daughters, which is his second coming'.

Like many others of his generation who entertained hopes of a change in society, Winstanley experienced disappointment (see 'New Year's Gift', Hill 1973: 205, and on the disappointment, Hill 1985). In its place came concern with inner transformation which provided a resource for that generation to seek for the light within and engage in an inner struggle, when the prospects for engaging in it, in the world at large, seemed to lead only to defeat. 'The experience of defeat' was to be the lot of many who looked for a new order.

As Hill demonstrates, Winstanley was not on his own. The Diggers were accompanied by the Ranters, the Muggletonians, the Seekers, the Levellers, the Familists, the Anabaptists, and many others, whose views were excoriated in the critique of writers like Thomas Edwards in his *Gangrena* and persuaded Thomas Hobbes that there was need of some kind of monarchical control to keep the lid on the Pandora's Box of popular religion.

There were many others, along with Winstanley, like Ludowick Muggleton and Abiezer Coppe, Anna Trapnel, Eleanor Davies and later Anna Wentworth and John Bunyan (to name but a few), who reflect this vital, antinomian world of English religion, which, as we now know, did not come to a sudden end with the establishment of Church and monarchy in 1660, but bred a wonderfully variegated underground movement, which contributed to the greatest radical writer of them all, William Blake. Looking back now I can see that Hill's book does not reflect adequately the vibrancy of women's writing. The discovery through a more recent Hill book, *The English Bible*, of relatively unknown writers like M. Marsin, as well as amazing prophetic figures like Anna Trapnel, and the subsequent illuminating studies of Phyllis Mack and Elaine Hobby, only reminds me of the important catalyst Hill's groundbreaking work was.

Mention of Blake demands that I explain why it is that I haven't chosen a book of Blake's or for that matter about Blake. The significant thing about the Hill book was that it was a key which unlocked so many doors, some of which I am still going through to explore the avenues that have opened up as a result. It is hard to overestimate the effect of discovering ideas such as are contained in Hill's book, and the inventiveness of the writing of the seventeenth-century radicals (the link is noted by Hill himself in an Appendix of *The English Bible*). On the one hand, my then growing interest in liberation theology enabled me to see that there were antecedents of a significant movement, which was attracting increasing attention in European and North American theology.

Several things were coming together in my theological and hermeneutical journey. I was struggling to find a publisher for a large book that I'd written on apocalypticism in ancient Judaism and Christianity, and what I was discovering in the seventeenth-century texts (which was subsequently confirmed by later research and writing) was that, far from being marginal to Christian theology, it had always been the motor for theological development. In particular, I had always doubted the way in which both exegetes and theologians had meekly accepted the Augustinian consensus about eschatology and regarded Christian hope as hope for another world. In what is an otherwise brilliant book, *The Pursuit of the Millennium*, Norman Cohn undergirds the prejudices of the theologically orthodox against the enthusiasts and the millenarians. But this, I became convinced, was endemic to Christianity, and I was then (and still am) convinced that I could not understand Christian origins without seeing it as a millenarian and apocalyptic movement through and through. Hill's book gave me a historical handle on that thesis, which enabled me to understand what had preceded and followed the revolutionary movements and ideas of seventeenth-century England. Winstanley, for example, was just one who believed that his actions were grounded in some kind of ecstatic experience, so that his convictions about the establishment of the Kingdom on earth was not some kind of 'pie in the sky' religion but something here and now.

More important than the academic stimulus was the way in which Hill offered me the beginning of a map of my nonconformist theology, something which was helped greatly by subsequent acquaintance with modern Anabaptists in Britain. One of the fascinating things that has occupied me in recent years is the underground mix of Anabaptist, millenarian and apocalyptic ideas in early modern English religion, which is the necessary seedbed for the work of Blake, not to mention Wordsworth and Coleridge. The research project I co-direct in Oxford, cataloguing and writing about the modern spiritual descendants of the late eighteenth- and early nineteenth-century prophet Joanna Southcott, has been a further exemplification of this extraordinary subculture in English religion.

The theological landscape has changed dramatically over the years since I first read Hill's book, perhaps as much as it did in the last decades of the seventeenth century. Then, as now, we see the emergence of a triumphant orthodoxy, though that orthodoxy has less and less impact on the majority of people in Britain, whether it be 'radical orthodoxy', or traditional Catholicism, or a New Age spirituality, which is out of touch with the political demands of the wider world. The kinds of concerns that led those like Winstanley to read the 'signs of the times', with the help of the apocalyptic images of the book of Revelation, seemed pertinent, even if the social and economic circumstances for the majority of the world's population had not improved. The witness of Winstanley in 1649–50 to a very different way of social relating and an understanding of society which was inclusive rather than preserving the entrenched privileges of the well off, was a *kairos*, an opportunity for change, for English society. The apocalyptic images of the book of Revelation were an appropriate way of understanding why things were as they were and the task which was required to 'build Jerusalem in England's green and pleasant land' (to quote Blake's famous words from a century or so after Winstanley), much as William Stringfellow had done in the crisis over the Vietnam war during the 1970s in the USA.

The funeral rites for liberation theology have been conducted by the wielders of ecclesiastical and political power for the last twenty years, especially since the fall of the communist regimes of Eastern Europe. But, as the veteran liberation theologian Jon Sobrino has suggested, if liberation theology has had its day, there is still the need for which the protest and articulation of that perspective first arose: the world of injustice, of Dafur, of the HIV-Aids in Africa and the massive discrepancies between the lot of the minority and the majority of the world's men, women and children. My colleague Ivan Petrella, in his timely book, *The Future of Liberation Theology: An Argument and Manifesto* (2007), has, in his analysis of the predicament of liberation theology, demonstrated that its genius is in its commitment to the emergence of a theology originating within specific social and political projects, both reflecting its contextual character and its roots in action for social change. This, not the various theoretical and culturally aware developments that have emerged in the last decade, is crucial and takes us straight back to Winstanley's 'action is the life of all'. Petrella not only grasped what is central in liberation theology but also what is necessary for any theology that is related to the project of the coming of God's Kingdom on earth. Implicit within the argument is the conviction of Vatican II (of course echoing Acts 2 and the prophecy of Joel) that the Spirit is poured out on *all* flesh, and that change is neither ecclesial nor apolitical, or for that matter merely inward or psychological. Liberation theology has put its finger on the pulse of the historical change, which is the work of the Holy Spirit, who makes all things new. It did this by realizing that theological understanding comes through the commitment and action and discernment, as a complement to that activity, not a replacement for it. All these together are part of the reading of 'the signs of the times' and the possibility of working for change, which discernment within the context of commitment to the poor and marginalized can offer. In recent years several commentators have sounded the death-knell of liberation theology. Even if liberation theologians have made some mistakes, they have identified something fundamental to the theological task: speaking of God in a world that is inhumane. Such a standpoint is a central component of any catholic Christianity worth the name, and it is necessary for a church seeking conformity with the way of Jesus to discern the standpoint of those who may be particularly well able to perceive Christ. Perhaps this is the most disturbing thing about the theological tradition that liberation theology represents: that there exists a hermeneutical privilege for the poor and marginalized, and a consequent loss of privilege and status in academy or church. As one English ancestor of liberation theology, Gerrard Winstanley, put it:

> Nay let me tell you, that the poorest man, that sees his maker, and lives in the light, though he could never read a letter in a book, dares throw the glove to all the humane learning in the world, and declare the deceit of it. ('New Law of Righteousness')

It may be a sign of age, but the experience of the last thirty years has made one thing central for me in the changed circumstances of a globalized economy. We must learn from the over-ambition of the radicals in the 1650s and not mistakenly hope for a humane, more equal, society and world and make it impossible by precipitate actions. While I do not think that Winstanley's project of digging the common land in 1649 was unrealistic politically, given the opportunity he discerned, he quickly realized that the supposed 'new age' was less the era of the reign of King Jesus than the reassertion of the privileges of the burghers of England, though without a monarchic head. Perhaps even the less ambitious aims of the Levellers were impossible (and one is reminded of Cromwell's purge of Leveller elements which led to the execution of the Leveller rebels in Burford churchyard in May 1649, which many of us now commemorate annually). My view is that 'never again' must we allow a right-wing government such as that presided over by Margaret Thatcher to win power, and that I will do anything (tactical voting being the most obvious thing open to me) to prevent that happening. I am no fan of Tony Blair or Gordon Brown, nor New Labour, but what has happened in Britain over the last 12 years is infinitely better than life under Thatcher.

Reading Hill's book again reminds me of the intellectual stimulus that was given by the discovery of the treasure trove of radical Christianity in England. What strikes me is that, despite the overt political commitments of Hill, his historiography is thoroughly imbued with a concern for what Blake termed 'minute particulars', rather than theoretical abstraction. It is a testimony to a way of engaging with the past, which is not theory-laden as is seen in so much contemporary academic discourse. There is something about Hill's evocation of the past that is understated, fascinating, and yet sympathetic, which I would be glad to emulate. What strikes me very forcibly again, as I read it, is what struck me when I first read the book, is that, *mutatis mutandis*, the seventeenth century captures the intellectual and social power of the history of the origins of Christianity. That applies both to those who espouse radical ideas and practise them as to their opposite, for it is the very paradox of the ways in which radical ideas and practice sit cheek by jowl with their contrary, social conservatism and conformity, and the longing to avoid causing offence, which characterises both early Christianity, as it does the story of theology in England in the second half of the seventeenth century.

Like many others of his generation who entertained hopes of a change in society, Winstanley experienced disappointment. Milton was to express this in his later writing as the hopes of political transformation became muted. Bunyan in *Pilgrims Progress*, like so many others, focused on the quest for individual salvation in a Promised Land beyond this world, which might compensate for the disappointments of never seeing it in this. Concern with inner transformation enabled a generation of 'the disappointed' to seek for the light within and engage in an inner struggle, when the prospects for engaging in it in the world at large seemed to lead only to defeat. The experience led some to political conservatism, as political realism offered a more appropriate paradigm of the exercise of political power than the democratic egalitarianism of the millenarians. The egalitarian spirit of the Quakers, in their conventicles and good works, kept alive a concern for inwardness and the eschewing of hierarchy and force. The silent protest against the status quo became the only possible strategy available to those who sought to keep alive the flame of hope, when the opportunities which seemed to be on offer in the 1640s seemed to have disappeared.

If no New Testament writers shaped the despair of Gerrard Winstanley, as he viewed the wreckage of his hopes, they would have understood what drove him to do what he did. Both the first Christians, and the seventeenth-century radicals, whom Hill writes about so eloquently, longed for, and believed they caught a glimpse of, the Kingdom of God on earth. It was Winstanley's task, however, to articulate the lot of the modern radical too, and to accept that New Labour (or its equivalent) is probably the best we can hope for as we attempt to resist the cataclysm of neo-conservatism:

> Here is the righteous Law, Man, wilt thou it maintain?
> It may be, is, as hath still, in the world been slain.
> Truth appears in Light, Falsehood rules in Power;
> To see those things to be, is cause of grief each hour.
> Knowledge, why didst thou come, to wound, and not cure?
> I sent not for thee, thou didst me inlure,
> Where knowledge does increase, there sorrows multiply,
> To see the great deceit which in the World doth lie.
> Man saying one thing now, unsaying it anon,
> Breaking all's Engagements, when deed for him are done.

O Power where art thou, thou must mend things amiss?
Come change the heart of Man, and make him truth to kiss:
O death where art thou? Wilt thou not tidings send?
I fear thee not, thou art my loving friend.
Come take this body, and scatter it in the Four,
That I may dwell in One, and rest in peace once more.

(Gerrard Winstanley, 'The Law of Freedom',
Sabine 1941: 600)

References

A. Bradstock (1998), *Faith in the Revolution*, London: SPCK.

A. Bradstock (2000), *Winstanley and the Diggers, 1649–1999*, London: Routledge.

A. Bradstock and C. Rowland (2002), *Radical Christian Writers: A Reader*, Oxford: Blackwell.

C. Hill (1972), *The World Turned Upside Down: Radical Ideas During the English Revolution*, London: Penguin.

C. Hill (1973), *Winstanley: The Law of Freedom and Other Writings*, Cambridge: Cambridge University Press.

C. Hill (1977), *Milton and the English Revolution*, London: Faber & Faber.

C. Hill (1978), 'The Religion of Gerrard Winstanley', *Past & Present* Supplement 5, p. 50.

C. Hill (1985), *The Experience of Defeat*, London: Faber & Faber.

C. Hill (1993), *The English Bible and the Seventeenth Century Revolution*, Harmondsworth: Penguin.

J. Kovacs and C. Rowland (2004), *Revelation: The Apocalypse of Jesus Christ*, Oxford: Blackwell.

C. Rowland (1988), *Radical Christianity: A Reading of Recovery*, Cambridge: Polity.

C. Rowland (1985, rev. edn 2002), *Christian Origins: An Account of the Setting and Character of the Most Important Messianic Sect of Judaism*, London: SPCK.

G. H. Sabine (1941), *The Works of Gerrard Winstanley*, Ithaca, NY: Cornell University Press.

6

EQUIANO'S *INTERESTING NARRATIVE*

Re-reading a Modern Scriptural Story

Vincent L. Wimbush

> It is . . . I confess, not a little harzardous, in a private and obscure
> individual, and a stranger too . . . to solicit the indulgent attention of
> the public; especially when I own I offer here the history of neither a
> saint, a hero nor a tyrant. I believe there are a few events in my life
> which have not happened to many . . . and did I consider myself an
> European, I might say my sufferings were great; but when I compare
> my lot with that of most of my countrymen, I regard myself as a
> particular favourite of Heaven . . .
>
> Olaudah Equiano's *Interesting Narrative of the Life of Olaudah
> Equiano, or Gustavus Vassa, the African. Written By Himself*[1]

I have learned that if we are fortunate, that is, if we live long
enough and with sufficient health and energy, we come to a
point of longing to tell our life story – primarily for ourselves,
only secondarily for others. I have approached that point: I
need to tell my story. I need first to find out how best to shape
it and the most compelling way to tell it.

This chapter is not about my story. But it is opportunity for
me to rethink a story that has for years, since my first encounter with it more than 25 years ago, puzzled me, haunted me,

---

1 From Olaudah Equiano (2003), *The Interesting Narrative and
Other Writings*. Ed. with an Introduction and Notes by Vincent Caretta,
New York: Penguin. Subsequent page references are to this edition.

confused me, tortured me, inspired me; and now it also helps me to construct and communicate my own story. At first reading, I was simply not able to go into the deep with the writer. I could not see in the luminescent darkness provided by the story. It was a painful experience; I found myself stumbling and falling around, with little or no sense of what the writer was exposing me to and challenging me to address, beyond and below the surface level. During the many years that have gone by I have learned the importance of learning to read in the dark and to read darkness. And so the return to the complex and disturbing story is altogether different. The story no longer sends me away in frustration or leaves me musing at the surface level; it now helps me to go down, downward to excavate and address the dark sites of memories that may constitute and help give shape to my story.

The story that I revisit is now the historical-discursive site that serves as entry point for the self-excavation that helps me with my story-telling work. It is the self-described 'interesting narrative' of the late eighteenth-century Black Atlantic figure Olaudah Equiano. *The Interesting Narrative of the Life of Olaudah Equiano or Gustavus Vassa, the African. Written by Himself* has, since its original publication in 1789, been read and interpreted for many different purposes and publics – in literary and cultural criticism; in eighteenth-century English social-cultural history; in the history of abolitionism on both sides of the Atlantic; and in African diaspora and slavery studies. In his story, Equiano positions himself as focal point of contemporary moral and political-economic crises brought on by violent conquest, disruption and enslavement. He figures himself as qualified insider ('almost an Englishman') having been outsider ('stranger'=slave) looking in, the one to whom initially the English books did not 'speak', yet one who is complexly in possession of – and becomes self-possessed in complex relationship to – the supreme (English) Book. Through his initially involuntary but later shrewd, strategic, voluntary travels by ship and his associations with other 'strangers' ('Indians') and ex-centrics (white religious dissenters and politicians), Equiano was able to make the books 'speak' to him and through his own writing 'speak' back to the constraining social and political structure. His story can be understood both as an 'epic' – a script-ur[e]-alizing – of life in the Black Atlantic diaspora and a 'founding text' of a more poignantly expansive Britain and United States.

Although Equiano was in many respects somewhat unusual in some of his experiences, he was – and remains – fairly typical of black folks' 'making do' with the North Atlantic worlds they have been made to undergo, whether slave or 'free' (the latter always and everywhere in the eighteenth century throughout the Atlantic worlds understood in highly qualified terms). Metonymic of the black-inflected vernacularization of the North Atlantic worlds, Equiano's story provides the outline for a layered history of Black Atlantic politics, representations, gestures, and mimetic practices.

Because I read my story in relationship to Equiano's story, I can understand my personal story as a 'scriptural' story. This is so precisely because Equiano's 'interesting' story can be said to be for the modern Black Atlantic world (to which I belong) a paradigmatic story. It is, as such, a 'scriptural' story in the most fundamental terms, not so much because it quotes from the Bible, but because it problematizes 'scriptures', as it presents itself as a reading of readings of scriptures. Most interesting and fundamental, Equiano's story is scriptural story because it is an epic story, a story about a great journey, a great struggle, about trauma and survival, about the fall into and away from 'sin', and about 'salvation' and transformation.

Equiano's story as scriptures is also not only or simply about the fate of one person or one people. It is really and complexly about multiple freighted matters and events – about the trauma of having been an abject outsider and transforming such status into survival and some success, using a black person in the North Atlantic worlds of the mid-eighteenth century to think with. More specifically, it is about: how a formerly enslaved black person comes to call himself 'African', 'Christian' and 'almost an Englishman'; about what such transformation of identification and identity and consciousness meant and means, what it entailed, what it assumed, what it required; and about how what is called 'the scriptures' or 'the Bible' – as a fraught catchphrase or abbreviation for a set of historical and ongoing phenomena and dynamics – is made to work in relationship to all of these events and phenomena. So Equiano's story is not *just* a story about any one people or tribe or any one person. The complexity and politics of even the author's name are registered in its title: he was known most of his life not by the name I use throughout this essay – Equiano – but by another name – Gustavas Vassa – forced upon him under the circumstances of enslavement. That his story provides two different names goes to the heart of the issue to be addressed in it, that is, identity formation. The story seems to be a pointed status-sensitive reflection – on the part of one who was a 'stranger' made to be a slave *because* he is black – about identity formation and about the quest for integration and power.

That such fraught issues are registered by a formerly enslaved black person of the eighteenth century is not to be taken lightly: for obvious reasons, few black people in the eighteenth-century worlds of the North Atlantic were expected to be able to speak and write in English (or in any of the other languages of the dominant peoples of the North Atlantic) about anything, much less about themselves to the extent and on the discursive-political terms represented by Equiano's book. Equiano may not have been absolutely unique, but he was, as the British were given to saying, a rare bird indeed. Yet Equiano's story is most 'interesting' for my purposes in this book not because of those rather rare and unique aspects of his life, but because of his story's rather sensitive articulations of some basic sentiments that had to do with the challenges, pains and traumas and survival strategies that characterized the existence of almost all black persons in the North Atlantic worlds. It is clear that the larger political circumstances placed different types of constraints upon him as a writer, and he seems at times to be sensitive about whether he was registering sentiments of all black peoples of his time. Nevertheless, I find that Equiano's registration of his experiences of identity formation and integration has become poignantly representative of most, if not all, black persons in the North Atlantic worlds of the mid to late eighteenth century – and far beyond. I contend that my story is included in the 'far beyond'. This is why I thought it not only appropriate but also provocative and potentially revealing of depths of complexity to name my story and Equiano's story as scriptural stories.

The way Equiano begins and frames his story is puzzling and fascinating. The story begins in Chapter 1 with Equiano assuming and reflecting the consciousness of his mature self – an African Christian who is 'almost Englishman' – looking back on what his native ('Ebo') peoples and their ways and traditions should mean to him and his (mostly sympathetic and mostly white British Christian) readers. In this looking back at the ways of his native world, and the significance of such, he attempts to communicate to readers what can be found not in the mind of the youthful Equiano of the world of the Ebo people inside the narrative and the narratological past, but in the mind of the mature story-telling, book-writing, talking-back-outside-of-the-narrative Equiano (the only mind that should be the object of the alert general reader and of critical scholarly reflection). It is in this first chapter of his story that Equiano creatively situates and defines himself and orients the reader: he names, describes and sums up all that he as writer understands himself to be and signals what is for him the point of his story-telling. He tries to take stock of, analyse and sum up those worlds that now define him – on the one hand, that 'world' into which he was born and which initially shaped him, the world of his own tribe, located in a part of what is now called Nigeria; and, on the other hand, the 'world' of the dominants in which he was first made a slave and 'stranger', into which he was later to some degree and with some success to be integrated. (It needs to be kept in mind that, according to some scholars, he may have been born in western Africa [Nigeria] and raised in South Carolina. At any rate, the point is that the chapter is focused on that world before or certainly different from the one in which he was made a slave.) The look back upon the world of his origins serves as Equiano's most forthright and ironically also most veiled message to his readers. Of course, the entire story is a look back. But with the somewhat descriptive, analytical, comparative religious and sociological analysis of the ways of the two different worlds embedded within his look back upon his origins, his first chapter frames the entire story, sets its tone and the message and structure;

everything is meant to be interpreted in light of it. In this chapter, Equiano communicates all that his story is about. The subsequent chapters represent the narrative, episodic unfolding of the message of this first chapter.

What is communicated in this first chapter is the message that, notwithstanding some fairly minor differences – for example, in languages and speech, certain customs, styles and traditions – between the world of the British and the world of the 'Ebos', they are similar in matters that are for Equiano fundamental and profound. That is, far beyond little differences in such matters as dress and quaint customs, in matters having to do with how these worlds are structured, how they are made to work, how sacred knowledge is mediated in them, and so forth, the two worlds are assumed to be very much alike. Such an assumption is obviously an important part of Equiano's agenda to bring his readers to a point of relativizing what he – again, as African Christian narrator – considers the big differences between the British people (and by logical extension all Europeans) and the black peoples now being called Africans (scattered throughout England and other North Atlantic worlds and in 'Africa' itself).

The matters most fundamental and profound around which Equiano thought there was similarity between the two worlds are really reduced to the one issue – the system or structure of sacred knowledge and the media by which it is channelled and the institutions and figures that control it. Equiano's narrative and his history of letter-writing and engagement in public debates make it clear that he was quite aware of the importance of recognizing and responding to the centres of power and their authorized representatives in British society. He clearly knew about the political structures of the British people: through his abolitionist associations he had some direct or indirect communication with a few members of Parliament. He also understood the power of communicating by letter with royalty and other powerful figures. But he also seemed to recognize how much even royalty and members of Parliament and other powerful officials – political, cultural, financial, ecclesiastical – in British society were affected and determined by what may be called the politics of a type of structure of media of knowledge and opinion. This includes the press, of course, and behind it the power that literacy in the now Protestant Britain represented. A more accurate understanding of what obtained in this situation may be that (the forerunners of) these officials at the top of the society really set up the arrangement and insured that they would continue to profit by it. At any rate, Equiano seemed to have learned how things were arranged, how things operated. He certainly figured out that what insured the current power arrangement was a set of assumptions held about a structure that framed and justified and secured the institutions and offices and traditions of power.

Somewhat in the manner of an early modern ethnologist, Equiano figured that at least one of the most important aspects of the structuring of authority and power in the Protestant British world should be seen to be in relationship to the facility for reading – that is, reading the book, *the* Book, the Bible, the (English) scriptures. The full story that Equiano tells has his character discover and take special note of the fetishistic (such an ironic twist here – the black person seeing the fetishizing practices of the British peoples). Even as all other (literary, religious) influences and factors are taken into consideration, Equiano's writing – the very (f)act of his writing – must be seen as the profound response to and negotiation of the British world. (This is the pointed meaning of the famous non-'talking book' incident that is included in his Chapter 3.) Whatever the promptings or influences on his decision to write his story, Equiano made the telling a quite fascinating response to the assumptions on the part of the British people about the capabilities of black peoples, especially as regards the engagement of *English* scripts and books, *English* expressions of ideas and sentiments.

Beyond the disturbing fact of his learning to read and write – that is, his learning to 'hear' the book 'talk' and his learning to 'talk back' to it and to the world of the book – Equiano made his story-telling a critical-analytical and political 'reading' of, a 'signifying' on, the British world. But his primary agenda in the writing of the full story seems to have been to fathom and critique this world, not for the sake of general inquiry or the mere curiosity of the explorer or the ethnologist, or even, in the tradition of the 'signifyin(g) monkey' (Henry Louis Gates), to upbraid and overturn it, but with the goal of better situating himself, integrating himself as part of (a redefined, reordered) English world.

The most salient and poignant comparison that is set up in Chapter 1 is between the British world (and, again, by extension, the dominant and predominantly Christian North Atlantic) and the world of his homeland in western Africa that has to do with the underlying operations and systems. Again, with the sensibilities of an early modern explorer or ethnographer/ethnologist, he notes that the most important operation by and around which the world of his birth and earliest years runs has to do with those persons he seems to recall (or remembers being told by others, according to oral traditions) are called 'Ah-affoe-way-cah' – priests/magicians/wise men:

> Though we had no places of public worship, we had priests and magicians, or wise men. I do not remember whether they had different offices, or whether they were united in the same persons but they were held in great reverence by the people. They calculated our time, and foretold events, as their name imported, for we called them Ah-affoe-way-cah, which signifies calculators, or yearly men, one year being called Ah-affoe. (p. 42)

Whatever the source of this information, it should be seen in the way in which Equiano understands how this other and earlier world really operated or was structured. It registers his understanding of the fundamentals and foundations – the real operators and the real operations within, behind and beyond the quotidian and surface activities and events – that made that Eboan world what it was. What Equiano's comparative description seemed, without much elaboration, to suggest, was that over periods of time through various means and measures and strategies the 'Ah-affoe-way-cah' interpreted for the people the way things were and also helped them to see what was to happen in the future. In other words, such figures secured and made clear the naturalization of the structure and order of things.

Equiano's discussion about the role and operations of the 'Ah-affoe-way-cah' would suggest that he understood them to be universal, that is to say, what they represented – structure, order – was necessary for and found in all worlds. The names of the operators and operations may be different from one world to another, but that there must be operators and operations for the ordering and centring of worlds was clearly assumed. He no doubt thought it important to recognize who or what was the centre, who or what was responsible for securing the centre and the centring work in each world. One might even assume that Equiano, along with most people, thought that without such operators and their operations only chaos would ensue, that being without such forces and operations was unthinkable. He has strong personal sentiments about what it means to be in a world without understanding such matters: in such a situation he would remain vulnerable and alienated and powerless, doomed to being outsider, a 'stranger', unable to negotiate the world.

The reason for the descriptive comparison of the ways and structures and orders of the two worlds as Equiano understood them was then not simply to relate the details and facts about the ways of the world of Equiano's origins. Not only was such a project not really feasible for Equiano, it did not square with his agenda. His agenda was to comment on the world of his origins only insofar as it provided a narratological set-up for his more extended commentary on his 'new' world, or the world in which he had been (made to be) a slave and a 'stranger'. Such extended commentary, that is, the story that his Chapter 1 with its sketchy comparative discussion sets up, was told in order to show the reader *that* he had and *how* he had overcome tremendous odds to become something other than 'stranger'; to establish his having become 'almost an Englishman', an African 'Christian', who could now read and write and in fact contribute to the spreading of the English-inflected faith; to analyse, critique and challenge British society; to provide a first-hand account of the slave experience; and to participate in the campaign for the abolition of the slave trade and on behalf of the plight of the 'poor Africans' throughout England and the Africans in his homeland. So the matter of how he overcame the odds to become what he was as an almost English-evangelical-activist-writer is the point of Equiano's full story.

Now we must go back to the point about the descriptions and comparative analyses in Chapter 1: they must be viewed as setting up the episodes that are unfolded in the full story. They must not be seen as mere apologetics, that is, as an attempt to help the reader to see Equiano's world of origins as proximate and thereby acceptable to the British world. There is no doubt that there is an element of this agenda and sentiment, as Equiano's language regarding 'strong analogy' suggests. But if this were all that was at stake for Equiano, his story would have been in his own time (and would continue to be) rather differently received: it would have been read as *mere* mimetics, *mere* apologetics, and as such derided or forgotten. It certainly would not have become the bestseller in Equiano's own time and continued even today to be read all over the English-speaking world.

The 'strong analogy' offers something more and other than this. The focus from the beginning of the story – but perhaps not unveiled as clearly until later in the story – is not on the world of Equiano's origins; it is on the British world, the world to which, about which, Equiano writes, the world in which he finds himself, the world that he has learned to negotiate. The full story is commentary on the British world, its operations and structuring – through the eyes and sensibilities and experiences of a 'stranger'. It is trenchant, poignant commentary by a 'stranger' who was such precisely on account of his having been enslaved. It is commentary by one who became an ex-slave only by dint of his persistence, wiles, strength, and on account of his understanding himself 'a particular favourite of Heaven', learning to 'read' the British world, especially the terms on which it understands, locates and mediates power, and especially sacred knowledge and the power it brings with it.

So what Equiano did in the first chapter of his story was to use some received traditions and perhaps some imaginings from literary influences about the arrangements of the world of his origins in order to compare them to what he as an historical figure had already experienced, what he as a figure in the narrative would experience, as 'stranger' in the North Atlantic worlds. Of course, Equiano understood that in the British world, and throughout the worlds of the North Atlantic, there were no 'Ah-affoe-way-cah'. And he got the point that 'Ebo' rituals were not respected in Britain. He nevertheless recognized the strategic political-narratological importance of setting up the descriptions and analysis of the ways of the 'Ebo': he set up the discussion about the latter into categories or points of reference for the sake of his (white Christian) British readers. This set-up allowed him in the subsequent chapters to describe and comment on the (white Christian) British world.

The world of the Ebos, according to Equiano, was not like the world of the British in that the former was, as an example of a matter that was somewhat superficial, without 'places of public worship' (p. 42). Yet in a respect most important, in the world of the Ebos there were nonetheless 'priests' (the 'Ah-affoe-way-cah') who are compared to the 'priests' of the British world and their assumed (not having to be stated for the reader) important offices and institutional machinery. He argued that the Ebo priests represented knowledge of how things came to be and by logical extension the meaning of things in the present and the way of things in the future. There is an assumption that the British priests represent that same sort of knowledge and power. Clearly, this was the stuff of serious comparative observation, conceptualization and theorizing.

Most important was what Equiano indicated were the powers of the Ebo priests and the operations they represented. He did not know details; perhaps he had read or had been told – by elders? – that they 'were held in reverence by the people'; that they were successful in 'healing wounds and expelling poisons'; and that they possessed powers of insight and knowledge that were intimidating and disturbing, beyond the ken of ordinary folk: they had 'some extraordinary method of discovering jealousy, theft, and poisoning . . . ' (p. 42). These powers and operations Equiano understood to make that world work. In the priests/magicians/physicians was concentrated power, having to do mostly with knowledge – of the sacred, of the foundation and centring of the world.

Although the (first-time unsuspecting) reader is not given all the clues or any elaboration in Chapter 1, Equiano's story, I now understand, makes clear that what the British had – as it were, beyond and below the officials and the grand political and religious institutions – instead of the powers of the 'Ah-afoe-way-cah', were books and their power to speak, to activate communication among those who were part of the world of books and the capacity on the part of all those who belonged to that world. And it is what Equiano saw in the British people's practices and engagements with books that taught him over a period of time to associate books, especially the Good Book – the Bible – with knowledge of the origins of things, with the ability to 'calculate' the times in the British world. Those who could read – even those who were not priests – were seen in this world of the book to be more knowledgeable and more powerful. Those who could not read were seen to be severely disadvantaged. Indeed, those who could read were understood to be more authentically British! And the closer one was positioned to books and to the Book the more powerful one was thought to be. Priests in the British world were certainly considered powerful; but also powerful were scholars, jurists, and so forth.

For this phenomenon, the structuring/ordering/centring around scripts, around books, reading, and the Book, Equiano had no name or category. The subject is not broached in Chapter 1. Beyond Chapter 1 there are references again and again to books, to reading, to the Bible, and how important they were in British society. Books and the reading of them were shown to be important to him as one who sought to be integrated into such society. His persistence, even obsession, in learning to read books in general, the Bible in particular, was one of the most important signs of his having become 'almost an Englishman'.

This lack of explicit naming of the phenomenon of the book ('talking') culture at the beginning of the story seems to me to be very much by narratological design – part of the narrative-dramatic build-up that shows how Equiano became a mature reader-writer-Christian-almost-Englishman. Certainly, as the story develops the reader can see much evidence of the view of British society as a book-reading, more accurately, a Bible-reading, society. But what the reader is provided in Equiano's Chapter 1 is only a brief description of the traditions of the writer's world of origins in relationship to sacred knowledge. The intention in this chapter seems to have been to establish the origins and orientation of Equiano's journey toward becoming a reader-writer of the sort who could be integrated into and even (with qualification and poignancy) model Britishness. By focusing on the 'Ah-affoe-way-cah' Equiano disposes the reader to accept his understanding of how that society is ordered and structured. The reader is alerted to Equiano's intentions here by the commentary he adds to his description of the work of the 'priests' of the world of Ebos that serves to explain their power and effects:

> They likewise had some extraordinary method of discovering jealousy, theft, and poisoning; the success of which no doubt they derived from their *unbounded influence over the credulity and superstition of the people* ... (p. 42; italics mine)

The commentary here is very significant. It reveals Equiano's understanding of what the figures mean in terms of the structuring of the society he claims as his world of origins. In his view that society is structured around the 'unbounded influence' that the 'priests' have 'over the credulity and superstition of the people'. What does he mean?

In a chapter in which much of the point was to set up 'the strong analogy . . . which . . . induce[s] me to think that the one people had sprung from the other' (pp. 43–4), this statement is striking. The work of the 'priests', which makes the world of the Ebos a 'success', is said to be structured on the basis of 'unbounded influence over the credulity and superstition of the people'. This is a rather astounding registration of critical psycho-social analysis, self-consciousness and positionality. On the one hand, as a massive mixed-genre literature on group psychology now provides evidence, only a person already psychically and socio-politically integrated and socialized into (one of) the early modern worlds of the North Atlantic would deem others – that is, any non-Europeans, non-Christians, especially sub-Saharan blacks/Africans – and their orientations and sensibilities in the freighted terms of 'credulity' and 'superstition'. On the other hand, only a person not yet totally or securely socialized or integrated into a particular world, including the British and other North Atlantic worlds, would have been sufficiently positioned at a psychic distance away from its centre in order to analyse it critically in terms of 'influence', whether understood as 'unbounded' or not.

Simply raising the issue of 'influence' and its extent was a radically critical breakthrough. What Equiano reveals with such commentary is, to say the least, a rather complex positionality and consciousness. He reveals his positionality and thinking to be *at once inside and outside the two worlds*. Within the context of his Chapter 1, the somewhat detached critical distance in his description of and commentary on the world of the Ebos, on the one hand, and his rather careful, nuanced and spare references to the British world and its ways, on the other, are a clear reflection of Equiano's agenda and of the identity of his readers. He cleverly, with considerable nuance and style, set up in Chapter 1, but developed and elaborated upon throughout the story, wants to move his white Christian British readers to see in him as one who has become a partial and qualified and sometimes disturbing mirroring and reflection of what they are, what they represent, a model carrier or translator of their ways, orientations, sensibilities. To a great (and for some readers then and now doubtless a frustrating and unnerving) extent Equiano thinks and writes as one of them! This is the reason there is little need in his Chapter 1 to describe and offer commentary about the ways and structuring of the British world. At the level of consciousness at which Equiano meets the reader in this chapter he presumes to be one of them. Here he most clearly does *not* reflect the consciousness and sensibilities of those who live in the world of the Ebos. He does not reflect the level of consciousness and sensibilities of the person who according to the story was born into that world and who has stolen away from it into North Atlantic slavocracy. No, it represents the consciousness and sensibilities of Equiano the African Christian, one who was 'almost an Englishman'. What 'almost' represents is very much to the main point of the entire story, which explains how it is that Equiano has the consciousness and sensibilities of one who is somewhat outside *and* somewhat inside the British world. This dual positionality and consciousness then provides the pretext and the agenda for the rest of the story. Beyond Chapter 1, Equiano goes on to explain how he became what he became as writer; and this necessarily means he has the opportunity and burden to offer some commentary on the ways and structure of the British world.

Equiano's Chapter 1, then, explains the ways and structure of the world of the Ebos as a kind of preface to the description of and commentary on the British world seen through the eyes of Equiano. The commentary on the British world is artfully done – it is almost misleading in its indirectness and subtlety and its slow build-up. But the characterization of that world in relationship to the challenges that Equiano faced is the focus of the story. To see Equiano's Chapter 1 as a description of, even a commentary on, the Ebo world as an end in itself is to miss the serious point and artfulness of the story. This would be a type of fundamentalist-tribal exegesis! Equiano's intention was to have the references to the world of the Ebos function as set up and framing discussion for the story about his interaction with the British world and his cultivation as an African Christian.

The characterization of the Ebo priests as having 'unbounded influence' over the people needs to be looked at more carefully. This could easily be understood as the type of hyperbole licensed by story-telling. But I think more is at issue here: 'influence' is a wonderfully chilling euphemism that seems to me to reveal to the reader Equiano's wry, creative and critical sensibility: what positionality must be assumed in order to think of the work of priests/magicians/shamans in any culture in terms of 'influence'? I have already indicated that the terms 'credulity' and 'superstition' locate Equiano as a condescending outsider critic of the world in focus. But I should like to argue further that these terms suggest that Equiano is commenting not so much on the gullibility and lack of critical skills of the people but on the structure that envelopes them and over-determines their thinking and actions. 'Unbounded' hints at an arrangement or situation that is rather powerful, beyond the capacity of ordinary folk to counter or undermine. Modifying 'influence', 'unbounded' here adds up to a structure that can hardly even be recognized for what it is in reality, much less gainsaid or overturned.

The description and analysis of the Ebos reflects Equiano's own version of an ideological (meta-) structure-alist thinking about the British world. He applied this structure-alist thinking in explicit terms to the world of the Ebos; he did not, for obvious reasons, perfectly balance it with the same kind of discussion – with description and commentary – about the British world. But the discussion in Chapter 1 about the Ebos nevertheless did set up the British world for an extended, complex comparison. Equiano discerned and explicitly discussed how the Eboan world was structured, what/where were the most powerful 'unbounded' 'influences' on the people; and he figured out where he needed to position himself in relationship to this structure. He does not elaborate on his thinking about the structure of the British world in direct terms; he shows us in the story how he – his character – discovered the structure and what he needed to do to negotiate it. As he does so he writes not as social scientist, at least not as one without disguise; he writes on the surface, as a story-teller, signifying all the way.

Given this perspective on what Equiano seems to have been doing and setting up in terms of the perspective on the two different worlds that his story brings into view, the comment regarding the 'unbounded influence' over the (Eboan) people takes on special significance. The language used seems almost anachronistic, as though Equiano had perspective on a situation from another time – a future time that affords a more detached critical perspective. Or it could be understood that his self-described status as a 'stranger' vis-à-vis the British world should also be applied with respect to the world of the Ebos. So there is a double irony: not only is Equiano spatially and temporally separated from that world, he is also psychically separated from it. Yet that very separation from the Eboan world afforded him a particular perspective on, and gave him a language and categories with which to comment on and negotiate, the British world.

The notion of 'influence' has implications far beyond the Eboan world. It suggests that Equiano had learned to think about worlds in complex, hypercritical terms: his thinking went below and beyond the surfaces. He was questioning, sceptical. 'Influence' would seem to indicate that he did not accept social arrangements as they were – as natural. Indeed, the term betrays an assumption of operations that result in make-believe, illusions of some sort. That such a term is used in the context of discussion about the operations of those understood to be 'priests', 'magicians' or 'physicians' is most telling: since these individuals were the ones in that world who by 'some extraordinary method' knew things others did not know and had insight into things that others could not possess. They, after all, held the key to, controlled the media of, sacred knowledge. So what Equiano was arguing about such individuals was that they had enormous power – 'success'. But the 'success' they had was not something that should be associated with breaking rocks or manipulating the weather, and so forth. No, the 'extraordinary method' that resulted in their 'success' should be associated with their capacity to convince the people, to manipulate their minds and sentiments in ways and to degrees that were established and sustained – that is, make people accept as natural, 'make do with', the larger order, structure and arrangements. What Equiano seemed to have discovered, and aptly applied first to the Eboan world, was the ability on the part of the priestly figures, as anthropologist Michael Taussig put it (*Mimesis and Alterity: A Particular History of the Senses* [1993]), to 'make-believe'. The latter must be understood as that which is referred to in terms of 'unbounded influence . . . of the people'. It has to do with the complex creation and establishment of a social-cultural matrix within which is a certain reality to which people are oriented.

As chilling and shocking as the terminology of 'unbounded influence' and the analysis of it in terms of 'matrix' and 'reality' may seem to the reader, it is important to understand that Equiano does not express discomfort or displeasure with the situation he describes. On the contrary, he views the situation with some detachment, and a somewhat paradoxical sense of nostalgia or romance if not apologetics. The Eboan priests are not characterized as being duplicitous hypocrites or shady swindlers who have succeeded in duping the people; they are understood as creative, powerful individuals filling roles and functions mapped out for them and so expected of them. Equiano's perspective on these figures opens a different critical-analytical window on to these roles and functions in society and culture in general. Through his 'sketch', a 'strong analogy' between 'Jews' (he does refer to 'modern Jews' (p. 44), but on the whole the discussion is about biblical Jews (see p. 43)) and (romanticized ancient, narratologically invented, not contemporary) Eboan Africans, the reader is, I think, deliberately led to wonder to whom these figures, their operations and their effects may be compared in contemporary societies. That Equiano was indeed thinking and arguing in Chapter 1 about the contemporary situation and its challenges, about how the Eboan priests and their operations may be identified and understood in the contemporary British world, is made clear enough in the context of discussion in which he pivots his 'sketch' away from ancient-biblical 'Jews' ('Israelites') and ancient-biblical-world Ebos ('Africans') to 'modern Jews' and 'Eboan Africans'.

> Like the Israelites in their primitive state, our government was conducted by our chiefs, our judges, our wise men, and elders; and the head of a family with us enjoyed a similar authority over his household with that which is ascribed to Abraham and the other patriarchs. The law of retaliation obtained almost universally with us as with them . . . we had our circumcision . . . we also had our sacrifices and burnt-offerings, our washings and purifications, on the same occasions as they had . . .
> As to the difference of colour between the Eboan Africans and the modern Jews, I shall not presume to account for it. It is a subject which has engaged the pens of men of both genius and learning, and is far above my strength . . . [The many attempts to address the issue] it is hoped may . . . remove the prejudice that some conceive against the natives of Africa on account of their colour. (pp. 44–5)

It could not be clearer to the reader that Equiano's bottom-line interest has to do with contemporary Africans in the North Atlantic and the challenges they face – including enslavement. That he at some points puts the matter in more delicate and indirect terms – 'difference of colour', 'the prejudice that some conceive against the natives of Africa' – reflects (ironically) his sensitivity to the sensibilities of his (white) readers. But he cannot sustain his delicateness of expression: he picks up a bit of sarcasm and irony as he reflects on one of the major issues behind the writing of his story:

> The Spaniards, who have inhabited America, under the torrid zone . . . are become as dark coloured as our native Indians of Virginia, of which I myself have been a witness. There is also another instance of a Portuguese settlement at Mitomba, a river in Sierra Leone, where the inhabitants are bred from a mixture of the first Portuguese discoverers with the natives, and are now become, in their complexion, and in the woolly quality of their hair, perfect negroes . . . Surely the minds of the Spaniards did not change with their complexions! (pp. 44–5)

In this same context he ratchets up the rhetorical heat as he addresses even more pointedly and passionately the irrationality of Western Christian anti-black prejudice and the subjugation and enslavement of black peoples:

> Are there not causes enough to which the apparent inferiority of the African may be ascribed, without limiting the goodness of God, and supposing he forebore to stamp understanding on certainly his own image, because 'carved in ebony?' Might it not naturally be ascribed to their situation? When they come among Europeans, they are ignorant of their language, religion, manners, and customs. Are any pains taken to teach them these? Are they treated as men? Does not slavery itself depress the mind, and extinguish all its fire, and every noble sentiment? . . . what advantages do not a refined people possess over those who are rude and uncultivated? Let the polished and haughty European recol-

lect that his ancestors were once, like the Africans, unciv-
ilized, and even barbarous. Did nature make them inferior
to their sons? And should they too have been made slaves?
Every rational mind answers, No. (p. 45)

At the very end of this chapter, Equiano includes what
becomes a rhetorical pattern in his story – a concluding section
that follows with something approaching scriptural exposition,
complete with quotations of passages. The scriptural passages
seem to provide the key to understanding Equiano's story.
Christian scriptures, translated by the British for the British as
a nationalist text, also function in Equiano's story to unmask,
unveil the most sensitive, controversial, painful and troubling
truths. They are used to communicate in other terms – terms
that are indirect and deflecting yet pointed because they communicate knowledge and insight that are supposed to matter
most – the knowledge and insight like that associated with the
Ebo priests.

Most important for Equiano, scriptures were 'used' because
he came to understand them to be fully implicated, perhaps,
as the most important underlying factor, in the structuring
and order of the British world. (The Anglican clerics and the
evangelical exhorters and the Ebo 'priests' were likely seen by
Equiano as reflections of each other.) So the reason to conclude
every chapter with references to and exposition of the Bible is
not so much because of a flat a-political assumption or argument about biblical authority. The 'unbounded influence over
the credulity and superstition of the people', which in Chapter
1 is explicitly identified with the Ebo priests, the reader is led
by Equiano to implicitly associate with or compare to the
reading of scriptures in the matrix that was the British world.
Equiano schematizes his story so that it makes plain the significance of scriptures – to every British citizen, and to himself. In
spite of the enormous odds and challenges and setbacks, with
every chance he gets the Equiano of the story seeks to learn to
read the scriptures. Only when he has learned to do so and to
understand them on certain terms (that is, evangelical) does he
become 'almost an Englishman', or an 'African Christian'. In
fact, the quest to learn to read the scriptures could appropri-

ately and fairly be said to be the theme of the story. At any rate, in his quest to learn to read the scriptures Equiano indicates his awareness that the key to understanding the structure and arrangements and terms of negotiation of the British world are in direct relationship to the scriptures. The latter may in his mind represent many things, but among them is his view that they are the key to the matrix that was the British world.

Equiano has no explicit term that he uses throughout his story to refer to what scriptures meant in or to the British world. If appropriate comparison is made between scriptures and (his description of) the operations of the priests of the Ebo world, then Equiano's interest in the story-telling that follows Chapter 1 concerned whether and to what extent scriptures were implicated in the 'influence' – 'unbounded' or not – that led to and was protective of the 'illusions', the 'make-believe', that accounts for the structures and arrangements of the British world. The term 'make-believe' is particularly apt not because it has to do with un- or sur-reality. It is constructed and it is real: it is *real*-ity precisely because it is layered and complex, operating above and below the usual levels of 'reality' and appearances. It is *real*–ity insofar as it is a reflection of some aspects of both coercion and assent, a reflection of different types and degrees of violence as well as different forms of the giving of credence.

Equiano's story seems to establish the Bible among the British as a matrix or structure within which and by which a reality is created and maintained. It is sustained in complex relationship to texts, and so begs to be complexly analysed – for example, through the creative, intellectually transgressive (also risky?) application of the ethnography and ethnology, the sociology, social history, politics/power dynamics, and social psychology of reading texts, befitting a reality that is ideological-discursive, social-political, social-psychological – real in every domain and sector of human life. But these are simply fancy categories for the persistent raising of sets of basic questions and issues about the human life that was his.

I take up his story because it raises basic but utterly disturbing and even threatening questions and issues – about the work of scriptures, about social formation, about the structuring of consciousness. It opens a window on to the formation of the British people and about the formation of black peoples in relationship to the British people and their scriptures. I read Equiano's story again and again because it provides a critical lens through which I can begin to name some of the questions and issues and problems having to do not simply *with* literacy or the capacity to read in general or even to read a canon or classic text of the society, but self-making in connection with a 'reading formation'.

Equiano does not name this phenomenon as such; he turns the reader's attention to the phenomenon through his narration of 'his' experiences and views. His story points out the phenomenon through his experiences as one who is both insider and outsider, both stranger and 'almost Englishman'. Equiano only raises the issue of the phenomenon; he does not make it less complex; he does not explain its origins; and he does not chart the course of its history. But he makes compelling the fathoming of the phenomenon. I identify with Equiano's positioning and consciousness – in social-political and intellectual terms – and with his lifelong effort to raise the issue of the ascetics of identity formation. His story has become my story.

Reference

Olaudah Equiano (2003), *The Interesting Narrative and Other Writings*, ed. with an Introduction and Notes by Vincent Paretta, New York.

7

RE-READING
NELSON GRABURN'S
'INTRODUCTION' TO
ETHNIC AND
TOURIST ARTS:

Cultural Expressions from the Fourth World

Daniel L. Smith-Christopher

In this chapter, I reflect on my earliest experiences reading social science literature in relation to biblical studies. In modern postcolonial analysis of biblical studies, I have noticed that one of the most common forms of 'intra-textual readings' occurs when scholars read biblical texts in dialogue with modern novels, especially novels from indigenous, Diaspora, or Developing World writers. Most recently, the significance of this kind of approach is discussed by Vítor Westhelle in his interesting essay, 'Margins Exposed: Representation, Hybridity and Transfiguration', which appears in a volume celebrating an early collection of essays gathered by R. S. Sugirtharajah in the late 1980s entitled *Voices from the Margin: Interpreting the Bible in the Third World*.

In contrast to this kind of cross-textual reading, however, I have often spent a great deal of time with sociological and anthropological literature. I acknowledge the obvious value in the work of colleagues who engage with the voices of creative fiction in their reading of biblical texts. In my case, however, I feel a tremendous debt of gratitude for the work of colleagues in social sciences as they attempt to understand the meaning and significance of a host of different varieties of social phenomena. In this essay, I hope to make clear some of that gratitude by selecting an essay that had a tremendously formative impact on my early work in Hebrew biblical studies, especially my continued fascination with the Babylonian Exile and the literature that can be associated with, and read through, those events. At the outset, I should clarify that I have no particular reason to suspect that my own reflections carry any particular importance. I am pleased to have been invited to participate with others in this project of thinking about the value of 're-reading' writings that we each found particularly helpful. However, I would add that it is not my thoughts that are important here – I simply hope to introduce some of the thought of Dr Nelson Graburn to fellow students of the Bible.

The context of my reading

When I began my research on the Babylonian Exile at Oxford in 1983, the way forward seemed perfectly clear. Start by reading Peter Ackroyd's *Exile and Restoration* (1972), Enno Jansen's work, *Juda in der Exilszeit* (1956), and Kurt Galling's *Studien zur Geschichte Israels im persischen Zeitalter* (1964), and 'off you go'. The historical events could be reasonably summarized as follows.

In 605 BCE, Nebuchadnezzar defeated the remaining Egyptian resistance to his imperial designs, after defeating Assyrian resistance in 610–609 BCE. After a period of time consolidating his rule in Babylon after the death of his father, Nabopolassar, Nebuchadnezzar returned to his western campaign and laid siege to Jerusalem in 597. Young King Jehoiakin, aged 18, surrendered, and a significant, though presumably small, number of people were taken into exile and the city of Jerusalem was spared. All the numbers that we have for exilic events in the Bible are based on 597, but it was probably a few thousand initially, including portions of the royal family taken as hostage

(2 Kings suggests over 18,000 but some would argue that this now seems somewhat high). Tax and tribute duties were presumably part of the surrender negotiations.

Nebuchadnezzar appointed the remaining son of Josiah (who may have been seen as an allied family as opposed to the Egyptian-appointed Jehoiakim) named Mattaniah as client ruler in Jerusalem, renaming him Zedekiah – the act of renaming being a standard symbol of subservient status irrespective of the actual name chosen. In his tenth or eleventh year, Zedekiah apparently joined an Egyptian-instigated revolt, and Nebuchadnezzar's armies returned to deal the final blow to Jerusalem and surrounding cities (587/586). Jerusalem was devastated and an unknown number were killed or taken as exiles. Although some semblance of a remaining governing structure was attempted with the appointment of Gedeliah at Mizpah, this collapsed from internal feuding among Judean factions, and life in Judea remains unclear until the beginning of the Persian interest after the conquest of Babylon in 539. Our evidence for life among the exiles, and of those back in the land, is minimal.

Under Persian support of some kind (the nature of which is currently a major issue of contention), some of the exiled Judeans returned to Palestine to reassert control and rebuild their destroyed shrine, and eventually, Jerusalem itself. We then begin a period of over 200 years until the conquests of Alexander the Great, living under the apparently relatively peaceful, though economically difficult (Neh. 9.36–7) and uninterrupted control of the Achaeminid Persians until the more turbulent events of Ptolemaic and Seleucid Palestine that followed the conquests of Alexander in 333.

So it seemed to me in 1983 as I began my work. The historical narrative was reasonably easy. It wasn't difficult to summarize the main events then, and this still serves as more or less a fair initial summary of some of the major events. Having said all this, however, trying to assess the historical importance, and related to this, the social, religious and political impact of the Exile was, and is, much more controversial than one might immediately suspect – much more than I suspected then, certainly.

The importance of the Exile, and its impact on the life and faith of ancient Israel, have certainly not been matters of universal agreement. For example, it is not difficult to illustrate the tremendous volte-face that has occurred with regard to modern assessment of the Babylonian Exile in the last century. One begins with Torrey, for example, who famously wrote in 1910 that the Exile, 'which was in reality a small and relatively insignificant affair, has been made, partly through mistake and partly by the compulsion of a theory, to play a very important part in the history of the Old Testament . . . ' (Torrey 1910, p. 285). Torrey's extreme doubts began a tradition of de-emphasizing the Exile which would continue to express (albeit not in the extreme terms Torrey used) certain elements of scholarly views about the Exile. This ambivalence about the significance of the Exile endured through much of the twentieth century, and until very recently was still an aspect of the minimal study of this period, and especially the events of the Exile. In 1986, for example, in the influential historiography of Ancient Israel edited by Hayes and Miller, H. Donner wrote:

> It is easy . . . to overemphasize the drastic and debilitating consequences of the fall of Jerusalem and the triumph of Babylonian forces. Various aspects of life certainly were greatly modified, but Babylonian policy was not overly oppressive.
> The exiles were not forced to live in inhuman conditions . . . [and] . . . remained free and certainly should not be understood as slaves. They would have been under no overt pressure to assimilate and lose their identities . . . (Donner 1970)

But there were signs of different opinions along the way. In his *Studies in the Book of Lamentations*, for example, Gottwald considered the reality behind the lamenting poetry to be worthy of notice, but his proposed 'severest test' would not be taken up as a worthy theme of analysis in biblical studies for decades:

If the enduring memory of events and their impact upon succeeding generations is the major criterion of historical importance, then there can be no doubt that the sequence of happenings from 597 to 538 were among the most fateful in all Hebrew-Jewish history. Is it far wide of the mark to recognize in the sixth century BC the severest test which Israel's religion ever faced? (Gottwald 1964, p. 19)

Opinions remained mixed for some time. An excellent indication of this is the ambiguity in Bright's influential *History of Israel*. On the one hand, Bright would write: 'Although we should not belittle the hardships and the humiliation that these exiles endured, their lot does not seem to have been unduly severe . . .' And yet two pages later, writes: 'When one considers the magnitude of the calamity that overtook her, one marvels that Israel was not sucked down into the vortex of history along with the other little nations of western Asia . . . ' (Bright 1981, pp. 345–7).

This ambiguous assessment was shared even by Peter Ackroyd, whose work on the Exile is still considered by many to be the major analysis of the Exile in the twentieth century in English, and a work that was written, as he himself states, in *conscious awareness of the neglect of the exilic and post-exilic periods in Biblical analysis* (see Ackroyd 1968, 'The Exilic Age', pp. 1–16). But even Ackroyd's work, which dealt with the Exile as its main subject of investigation, reflected an ambiguity about the social conditions of imperial conquest and thus the circumstances of the people experiencing the Exile. In his assessment of the conditions of the exiles in Babylon, for example, Ackroyd writes that indications:

are of reasonable freedom, of settlement in communities – perhaps engaged in work for the Babylonians, but possibly simply engaged in normal agricultural life – of the possibility of marriage, of the ordering of their own affairs, of relative prosperity. (Ackroyd 1968, p. 32)

Yet, a few lines later, Ackroyd acknowledges that the 'uncongenial nature' of the situation should not be 'understated'. While each of these, in turn, attempt to present a balanced picture, the presumed 'lack of evidence' seems inevitably to push the scholars toward a benign assessment of the human and social impact of the Exile. A more severe impact, it seems to be presumed, would have left more evidence. That evidence would not be long in coming.

In his most recent survey of the question, Oded Lipshits provides what I believe is a more careful assessment of what we can know from the archaeological summaries available. It is instructive to note the radical change in tone in recent writing about the exilic events. For example, Lipshits refers to evidence of 'Nebuchadnezzar's desire to eliminate Jerusalem as a religious and political center' by burning the centres of government and religious ritual, the 'house of the Lord', and 'house of the King' (Lipshits 2005, p. 80).

Lipshits analyses a variety of indicators – the lists of people and their locations in Ezra-Nehemiah, the proposed borders of the provincial system of Yehud, and the archaeological distribution of seals, pottery styles, and destruction patterns. His work is especially important when he summarizes settlement patterns and population centres in the late Iron Age, and compares this with what we can know about the Persian Period. 'The first conclusion that arises from the survey data is that between the Iron Age and the Persian Period there was a sharp decline – more than 90 per cent – in occupation in the environs of Jerusalem' (Lipshits 2005, p. 218). He concludes: 'The demographic evidence thus supports the previous hypothesis that Jerusalem remained desolate throughout the time of Babylonian Rule' (Lipshits 2005, p. 218). The notion of an empty land seems mythical – but the notion of an empty Jerusalem seems anything but mythical.

Lipshits estimates that the total population of Judah at the end of the Iron Age was 108,000, and at the beginning of the Persian Period is 30,125 and concludes this section of his significant work as follows:

These demographic analyses have great significance for reconstruction of the history of Judah between the seventh and fifth centuries BCE, because they cast a different light on the biblical descriptions that, until now, have served as the primary, virtually exclusive source for all historical research. Thus, for example, it appears that the destruction of Jerusalem and the end of the Kingdom of Judah brought about the gravest demographic crisis in the history of the Kingdom of Judah, with much more severe results than the Sennacherib campaign of 701 BCE. The Babylonians concentrated their effort on Jerusalem and its environs, while the region of Benjamin and the northern Judean hills were hardly touched and continued almost unchanged in terms of settlement patterns and demography (Lipshits 2005, p. 270).

We have travelled a long way indeed from Torrey's 'insignificant affair' to arrive at the beginning of Rainer Albertz's sweeping history of this time-period, whose English edition opens with the following assertion: 'Of all the eras in Israel's history, the exilic period represents the most profound caesura and the most radical change. Its significance for subsequent history can hardly be overstated' (Albertz 2003, p. 1).

This significant change, however, was still at least a decade away when I began my own work on the exilic period. What I was most interested in was some kind of approach to the biblical texts (again, a literature more limited, I thought then, than today's tendencies to date a great deal more of the Hebrew literature in the exilic and post-exilic periods) that attempted to come to terms with the human events themselves, precisely because the texts are religious artifacts. Also, I was (and remain) convinced that a more enriched appreciation of religious expressions are gained when they are understood within the social and political contexts of their suggested times of production. Meaning, in short, is socially constructed.

It was hardly surprising that I found the few direct discussions of the Exile to be largely devoid of any attempts to assess the *extent and meaning of the human crisis itself*, largely because of a textual-critical bias toward measuring human impact only on the theological changes, or lack of changes, found in the text. Simply put, few texts spoke directly of the conditions of Exile, so it was determined that nothing can be said about such conditions.

However, theological change is itself a socially configured

language, so my own work on the sociology and social psychology of the exilic events was taken up in the light of what I saw as not only an inability to deal with, but a methodological avoidance of, the social, economic and cultural assumptions behind the lack of discussion on these matters of biblical literature. It is important to acknowledge, however, that many colleagues in a variety of areas related to this time-period in biblical studies have certainly made up for lost time! There are now a variety of debates that attempt to address the social, cultural, and political implications of what are perceived to be 'exilic' or post-exilic biblical literature – which, as I indicated, is today a considerably larger body of texts.

My own approach was to go beyond the use of non-biblical documents and archaeological reports, and try to learn more about the experience of deportation and resettlement itself. Thinking about these social phenomena (sadly, comparative cases are all too plentiful) would hopefully allow a more imaginative use of biblical texts read in the light of what we know about refugee studies, disaster studies, postcolonialist reflections, and sociologies of trauma. I am well aware that this last sentence amounts to a major 'red flag' in the eyes of many colleagues in biblical studies. Not only are other historical cases 'quite different in many ways', I was also warned endlessly that the very act of comparison would introduce bias in my analysis that could be avoided, presumably, by simply sticking to the texts.

My reply was always the same – it was (and is) too late for that. I was already deeply infected by the sociological observation that meaning is socially constructed. Debates in sociology about the 'social construction of reality' had long since convinced me. In other words – there is no such thing as 'sticking to the texts'. We all bring assumptions and presuppositions to the reading of historical texts – we all have imaginations that we draw upon to try to fit texts into a meaningful social reality. Virtually all of the observations I cited above from twentieth-century biblical scholars clearly presumed an imagined social reality of the Exile (even as they argued that there is a lack of clear evidence – indeed, *especially* when they claimed a lack of evidence). Imagination in historical analysis is unavoidable.

We might as well face the reality of social constructions, and at least attempt to 'train' our bias and assumptions to be armed with a wider ensemble of social possibilities and formations to draw upon.

The fact of the matter is this: most twentieth-century European and European-American assumptions with regard to social processes were brought to biblical studies from a study of classical civilizations, which is why 'comparisons' to Greek and Roman social formations were so readily at hand in previous work. Add to this the apparently convincing argument that Greek and Roman literature was not as far removed from Ancient Israel both geographically and temporally as a good deal of other available anthropological and sociological case studies, and the ease with which those classical social formations were cited begins to make some sense. The assumptions of classical social formations, however, were themselves rarely examined critically (as Holloway has so forcefully shown in his analysis of how British imperial notions influenced the interpretation of imperial Assyrian texts in British academic writing; see Holloway, 2002).

Before I turned to the social science literature that has informed my analysis in recent years, however, I was quite confused about a clear path toward developing a 'sociology' of the Babylonian Exile (though I readily admit that many consider me still to be very confused). Simply reading social science literature about displaced peoples was, perhaps naively, the way that I wanted to proceed. A significant step forward, however, was my reading of Nelson Graburn's programmatic 'Introduction' to a 1976 collection of essays that led not only to my realization of the pitfalls of a simple social science comparison, but alerted me to issues that led directly to my fascination with contemporary 'postcolonial' theoretical debates in relation to biblical studies. All the more interesting, then, to note that Graburn's work would probably strike him as far removed from biblical studies as a social scientist's work could be. Happily for me, I paid little attention to disciplinary boundaries then as now.

Meeting Graburn's work

After my initial year at Oxford working under John Barton with important advice from sociologist Bryan Wilson (of blessed memory), I returned to my home town of Portland, Oregon and determined to begin a serious number of months' reading in the very good holdings in anthropology of the Miller Library of Portland State University before returning to Oxford. While in Portland, however, I decided to ask the advice of the late Wayne Suttles, whose work on Northwest Native American language and culture is now legendary in his field. It had occurred to me that his work on Native peoples suggested the possibility that he may have some analogous cases to recommend to me – cases of Native 'relocations' that might prove interesting for a comparative study. His suggestion, however, rather befuddled me at the time. He listened to the outlines of my very rough thesis, and then said: 'Do you know the 1976 work of Nelson H. H. Graburn, entitled *Ethnic and Tourist Arts*? I think you would find this very suggestive . . .'

Tourist arts? I remember walking away from that interview wondering if Dr Suttles had heard me right, or was too busy to have paid me much attention. Neither impression was correct – he heard me quite clearly, and helpfully anticipated where I was headed in my analysis by suggesting the work that I now re-read. Along with expressing my gratitude to Prof. Graburn for his work, I would like to acknowledge my appreciation for the late Dr Suttles' insightful suggestions.

Nelson Graburn is an anthropologist who continues his work at the University of California in Berkeley, and whose work has especially focused in recent years on 'tourism' as a social and symbolic phenomenon with significant meaning in modern history. This later interest, however, appears to have grown out of his earlier interest in 'the anthropology of art', or what would probably be called today the study of 'social artefacts' within 'cultural studies'. His edited collection of essays, *Ethnic and Tourist Arts*, was one of the earliest expressions of this interest in the study of the symbolic and social 'meanings' of modern 'ethnic arts' and especially the interaction of these artefacts with 'tourism'. We would say today, I propose, that he was interested in the meaning of various locations of post-colonial contact, where 'ethnic arts' would represent a clear 'border interaction' between social groups of unequal power. In fact, how Graburn's work anticipated many of the insights and much of the significance of postcolonialist analysis is the main point of my reflections in this essay.

Re-reading Graburn

One must keep in mind that date of 1976 for a full appreciation of Graburn's ideas as outlined in his 'Introduction' to *Ethnic and Tourist Arts: Cultural Expressions from the Fourth World*. He states therein that he began to think about the various issues represented in this 'Introduction' as early as 1959. While many of these ideas have been expanded and expounded in many discussions since that time, especially in the context of 'postcolonial' social and literary theory, Graburn's opening essay articulated a number of key concepts that assisted me to conceive of the many ways to read biblical texts (as religious artefacts, as 'art') associated with the Babylonian Exile as a sociological event before some of the most recent and helpful articulations of postcolonial methods of reading the Bible. Graburn began by articulating the importance of his use of 'Fourth World':

> The Fourth World is the collective name for all aboriginal or native peoples whose lands fall within the national boundaries and techno-bureaucratic administrations of the countries of the First, Second, and Third Worlds. As such, they are peoples without countries of their own, peoples who are usually in the minority and without the power to direct the course of their collective lives (Graburn 1976, p. 1).

Graburn's identification of a unique set of circumstances for peoples who are surrounded by dominant cultures was a helpful clarification of what kinds of social circumstances are likely represented in the issues facing Babylonian exiles. Today, our articulation of the various 'locations' of analysis have divided these 'realities' into much more nuanced descriptions – but at least the idea of 'Fourth World' clarified an important difference between internally colonized peoples, and other forms of interaction involving the crossing of international boundaries. Graburn identified the unique circumstance of a border that entirely surrounds a people – they are 'captive'. So, first and foremost, a helpful clarification of the context for analysis.

What I believe is most significant about Graburn's approach as I now reflect on it, was his emphasis on interaction and mutual influence between dominant and subordinate cultures who are in contact in this kind of circumstance. Oppression, economic exploitation, racism, resentment – none of these typical dynamics of anti-minority attitudes prevents some level of interaction from occurring, even on the level of influencing expressions of indigenous culture. My later reading of Memmi's *The Colonizer and Colonized* would add considerably to this insight, but only by teasing out more nuances of Graburn's initial observations. Furthermore, Graburn explicitly acknowledged the host societies' interests in the 'primitive' among their own minority cultures as driven in many cases not so much by genuine interest in the minority cultures themselves, as by an exotic escape from their own alienated, industrialized anomie. Here was a significant indication of what would become Graburn's more recent work on tourism, which, though fascinating, is beyond the scope of this essay which focuses on Graburn's earlier work.

An aspect of the appeal of Graburn's analysis, I confess, was that I recognized myself. Though a European-American raised in what was then middle-class Southeast Portland, Oregon (a neighbourhood that is now much more economically distressed), I was the third son of hard-working Quaker parents who supported a family through a corner drug-store – itself an institution largely vanished from the American landscape. The Quaker identity always made me feel unusual, different and 'minority'. Thus, I have for some time had a fascination with 'Outsider art' (e.g. surrealism, or folk painting), 'vernacular architecture' (e.g. old Quaker meeting-houses as architectural protest), 'marginalized languages' (e.g. Yiddish), and the oral history of marginalized groups. I hadn't connected, consciously, the politics of my own marginalization as a leftish Quaker with what I perceived as aesthetic tastes. My own reality was and is socially constructed, as was (and is) my hermeneutics of scripture. I see this more clearly now. Not so much then.

I considered the most important contribution of Graburn's analysis to be his insights into the production of ethnic arts for tourist consumption. What I perceived, initially, as a straightforward case of exploitation of minorities by a dominant population's desire for a souvenir of the exotic, was revealed to be a far more complex exchange in Graburn's analysis. Stated simply, Graburn suggested that there are significant differences between the artefacts made for those within a group, for their own uses, and arts produced for others, for example, 'tourist arts'. Such production suggested a conscious strategy of managing social 'boundaries' among minority cultures that directly inspired my interest in religious and ritual strategies as evident in exilic-era ritual texts such as those represented by Leviticus and Ezra-Nehemiah. What James Scott so powerfully explored in his later, and now widely cited, books such as *Weapons of the Weak*, Graburn had introduced to me through his analysis of the managed interactions between 'First' and 'Fourth' worlds.

Not only did I learn to NOT trust initial 'obvious' impressions of what an artefact is, and thus what a biblical text 'says', I learned to honour the sophistication and resilience of 'poor' and 'weak' people who are 'defeated'. This kind of hermeneutic of respect (that is, presuming that people are capable of resistance other than violence, and such resistance can be culturally and socially very powerful) transformed my reading of the stories of Daniel, much less a good deal of other textual traditions associated with the Exile. But this is not the only line of Graburn's analysis. He was also interested in the changes that 'border contacts' introduce into the 'ethnic arts' themselves.

Graburn provided examples of the kind of influence on 'native arts' that are the subjects of the essays published in the collection he introduced. For example, indigenous artists can come into contact with new materials – new brushes, new beads, new paints and dyes, which can then be incorporated into Native artistic expression. But interaction can lead to new tastes and aesthetic judgements as well. European dress became adopted by New Zealand Maori as a sign of status within the Maori community, not necessarily as a request for recognition among European ('Pakeha') communities in New Zealand. The levels of analysis in these cases can be controversial. Are the Maori engaged in 'false consciousness'? Or are they engaged in genuine and independent 'indigenous' creative thought and decisions? Is independent thought possible in postcolonial contexts? As Director of our university's 'Study Abroad' programme in New Zealand, I can now speak from direct experience that it is impossible (not to mention unwise) to accuse the Maori of any inabilities to think or speak for themselves. A more sophisticated, resistant and resilient indigenous 'Fourth World' population would be hard to imagine. Maori scholars have long since dealt with, incorporated and analysed the European impact on their own cultural expressions – and the ongoing impact and creative response that continues.

The point is this – taking themes, ideas, artefacts, from more dominant cultures is not necessarily destruction of culture. Cultures, Graburn has taught me, are often more resilient than we think – and lines of resistance are often more subtle than we realize. The most striking page I read in his 'Introduction' essay is Graburn's attacks on snobbish judgements by outsiders on indigenous artistic forms and genres:

> But not all change is destruction . . . as outsiders we might not like such phenomena, or bemoan the 'lack of tradition'. But this *is* tradition; it is as real to the peoples now as the spirits of skulls and amulets were to their ancestors one hundred years ago. If Eskimos [sic, as Graburn himself now writes, the term is now Inuit] are Christian, they want to make crosses and altar-pieces for themselves, as they used to make ivory-tooth charms. When the Navajo made textiles for themselves and for local consumption (and not for the national collectors' market) they made them to their own liking, with imported bright cochineal and indigo dyes and unraveled bayeta . . . it is only recently that outsiders taught them to find and use muted, local natural dyes . . . (Graburn 1976, p. 13).

I remember going over those words again and again: 'Not all change is destruction . . .' Graburn trenchantly observed: 'European and Western society in general, while promoting and rewarding change in its own arts and sciences, bemoans the same in others . . .' (p. 13). Graburn wrote about cultural consumption by the majority societies as part of their alienation from their own social mores: 'The commercial fine arts are generally those demanded – more as status objects than as memorabilia – by people who wish to get "close to the native spirit" (not body of course) by having "genuine", "authentic" artifacts to show.' This, Graburn observed, often forces indigenous or minority artisans to conform to some historically frozen aesthetic in their own work in order to maintain economic benefits. Further 'market forces' push artisans to work on objects that are smaller size (transportable by tourists), less expensive (to compete with plastic knock-off imports of similar items). But there is evidence of what James Scott would later call a difference between 'scripts' – the indigenous artisans can either resist such dictation from market pressures, or manipulate these forces by producing intentionally constructed 'knock offs' for the market, without considering them to have anything like the value of what they would consider to be the 'real thing'. Clearly, there are strategies at work in aspects of production.

Finally, Graburn also talked about the intentional revival of archaic identities as a conscious strategy. This becomes a nuanced phenomenon. On the one hand, one can blame market forces for 'dictating' an aesthetic that is desirable to the majority, dominant cultures. On the other hand, the subordinate minorities can intentionally produce what appears to appeal, precisely because it does appeal, and thus becomes symbolic of their continued creative and strategic existence and identity. The artisan thus uses market forces to accomplish something of their own ends, even if it involves negotiations and changes. Artisans, therefore, in Graburn's terms, are not always 'reduced' to commercialism – the circumstances depend entirely on the meaning invested in the production by the artisans, and their cultures. While it is possible, Graburn asserts, for a complete 'sell-out', where the artisans are disempowered in the entire exchange and their entire involvement is dictated beyond the ability of the artisan and his/her culture to make any choices whatsoever, this is not always a complete assessment of the circumstances.

An excellent example of the interaction involved in such dominant–subordinant commercialized negotiations is the case of 'borrowed identities' in Graburn's analysis. In a three-step process, Graburn speaks of items (artefacts or raw materials) that are first borrowed, then incorporated, and finally offered to outsiders in their transformed state as an authentic representation of the culture that has incorporated these materials into their own creative processes. Can one imagine Palestinian culture without coffee? Yet this is an incorporated material that, once incorporated, became surrounded with 'native' production of containers and cups, but also social practices (chilli pepper in India?).

A further interesting example of the negotiations over commercialized indigenous motifs is the appropriation of artistic motifs and symbols by dominant cultures drawing on their Fourth World peoples. New Zealand, for example, draws heavily on Maori artistic motifs and traditions to represent, now, New Zealand as an entire society and nation. Australia uses Aboriginal motifs in national symbols. The United States routinely uses and displays Native-American thematics. But, as Graburn points out, it is simplistic simply to dismiss this as oppressive exploitation. It can certainly involve this – but there can be a level of co-operation in this appropriation, as an 'exchange' that is perceived to lift the status and identity of the indigenous peoples as essential players in the larger society. The negotiations involved in such relationships, obviously, are complex and varied. Graburn's warning to me then, and his warning today, is to be careful about drawing conclusions based on the force of a particular theory or ideology. Things are not always what they seem. A simpler statement capturing some of the force of postcolonial analysis would be hard to create.

As noted, much of this kind of 'negotiated' levels of interaction between dominant and subordinant groups within societies today forms a critically important aspect of postcolonialist analysis. Albert Memmi and Frantz Fanon, as writers of what would become classic texts in what is now called postcolonial analysis, revealed complexities of interaction that resist simplistic analysis into 'good guys' and 'bad guys', the disempowered and the empowered, the liberated and the self-liberating, the despairing and the resisting.

As I have indicated, these issues are best represented today in James Scott's analyses of minority resistance where he clearly questions the overriding, simplistic assumptions (often informed by a wooden Marxist grid, or a just as fossilized liberal grid) that propose that there are two realities – total self-governance, or total subservience, and where one does not find open conflict, there must be total capitulation. In other words, if bullets are not flying, if swords are not swinging, then there is total subservience to be bitterly condemned, or self-governance to be praised.

Such binary ('Manichean') and simplistic conceptions were not a part of the nuanced analysis of interactional social realities such as those proposed by Graburn, yet I found that they had governed biblical analysis in many ways – and it was crystal clear in relation to the issues raised by the Babylonian Exile. For example, if the Hebrews are not shown in plain, obvious resistance to Babylonian or Persian rule, then they were either totally defeated, or actually in favour of their imperial rulers. No open rebellion means no sense of subservience or loss. The nearly ubiquitous statement by biblical scholars before the 1980s that the exiles in the Babylonian heartland were 'not slaves' falls precisely into this category. Because the exiles did not call themselves slaves, or were not legally considered slaves in Neo-Babylonian social terminology, this was taken prima facie to indicate a reasonable if not always favourable status. This, then, deeply coloured the interpretation of texts such as the books of Daniel and Esther, representing the 'folklore' of the exilic experience.

I have suggested, however, in my own work on Daniel, that evidence of resistance, expressed partly in carefully negotiated levels of interaction, is a central theme of the Daniel legends and represents a far more nuanced way to interpret the significance of these texts. This interpretation was offered, however, in the face of a very common conclusion that the Daniel stories reveal the 'congenial nature' of Jewish existence under the Babylonian and Persian regimes.

Concluding observations

Nelson Graburn was talking about 'ethnic arts' as artefacts produced for the market – but he was also talking about the location of interactions between dominant and subordinate cultures. What he suggested was that these 'artefacts' need to be carefully 'read' in order to appreciate various levels of their meaning in the context of those interactions. Many of these ideas are now standard aspects of postcolonial analysis, post-modern analysis, and various forms of the 'deconstruction' of texts, including biblical texts.

I am in the interesting position, in relation to Graburn's work, that he has himself also engaged in a reflection not unlike my own here. In a concluding essay to the 1999 collection, *Unpacking Culture: Art and Commodity in Colonial and Postcolonial Worlds* (Phillips and Steiner 1999), Graburn was himself asked to reflect on his work on *Ethnic and Tourist Arts* published nearly 25 years previously. Not surprisingly, he acknowledges that the discussions of art and commodity have become a part of the larger debates in postcolonial analysis in modern work (and represented by the essays in the 1999 volume). I was particularly struck, however, with the provocative thoughts assembled in the following two paragraphs toward the end of his 1999 essay (I have omitted only his references to the essays within the volume itself):

> For analytical purposes we may state that there are always three agents involved in the production and consumption of hybrid arts in complex societies: artist, middleman, and consumer. It is, of course, the middleman who imposes the specific predicament on the artists. When the artists and the consumers are culturally, geographically, or temporally far apart, the mediating agent assumes greater importance. It is he or she who not only transmits the physical art object

from the producer to the consumer but who also controls the important flow of information about the object's origin, age, meaning, and producer . . . This includes important information about the status of the artifact as commodity or treasure . . .

Equally important in most circumstances is the function of transmitting back to the producer the demands of the marketplace and the ideology of the collectors. Such information may be transmitted merely in terms of price or repeat orders, or as specific information about form, content, color, materials, and so on . . . (Graburn 1999, p. 349)

All we need do, if my reader is not already a step ahead of me, is substitute 'Bible scholar' for 'middleman', 'biblical text' for 'hybrid arts', and the various institutional or theoretical academic constructs as 'consumer', and we are once again challenged by Graburn to consider the fascinating nuances of the contemporary contexts of biblical analysis. Perhaps it was, and is, my constant fascination with Graburn's analysis, as originally suggested by Suttles, that has engendered in my own work a strong resistance to disciplinary boundaries. Graburn may be talking about art, but it led me to think about biblical analysis in radically new ways – and guided me into the company of colleagues clearly more clever than I am, who now deal with postcolonial analysis within biblical studies. Many of us required an 'entry' into these discussions. I remain grateful that my entry was Nelson Graburn's fascination with tourism and artistic production as a legacy of cross-cultural contact.

References

P. Ackroyd (1968), *Exile and Restoration*, Philadelphia: Westminster.

R. Albertz (2003), *Israel in Exile: The History and Literature of the Sixth Century B.C.E.*, Atlanta: Society of Biblical Literature.

J. Bright (1981), *A History of Israel*, 3rd edn, Philadelphia: Westminster.

H. Donner (1970), 'The Separate States of Israel and Judah', in J. H. Hayes and J. M. Miller (eds), *Israelite and Judean History*, Philadelphia: Westminster, pp. 381–434.

F. Fanon (2004), *The Wretched of the Earth*, New York: Grove.

K. Galling (1964), *Studien zur Geschichte Israels im persischen Zeitalter*, Tübingen: Mohr.

N. Gottwald (1964), *Studies in the Book of Lamentations*, Naperville: Allenson.

N. Graburn (1976), 'Introduction', in N. Graburn (ed.), *Ethnic and Tourist Arts: Cultural Expressions from the Fourth World*, Berkeley: University of California Press, pp. i–xv.

S. W. Holloway (2002), *Assur is King! Assur is King! Religion in the Exercise of Power in the Neo-Assyrian Empire*, Leiden: Brill.

E. Janssen (1956), *Juda in der Exilszeit*, Göttingen: FRLANT.

O. Lipshits (2005), *The Fall and Rise of Jerusalem: Judah under Babylonian Rule*, Winona Lake: Eisenbrauns.

A. Memmi (1965), *The Colonizer and the Colonized*, Boston: Beacon.

R. B. Phillips, and C. B. Steiner (1999), *Unpacking Culture: Art and Commodity in Colonial and Postcolonial Worlds*, Berkeley: University of California Press.

J. Scott (1985), *The Weapons of the Weak: Everyday Forms of Peasant Resistance*, New Haven: Yale University Press.

J. Scott (1990), *Domination and the Arts of Resistance: Hidden Transcripts*, New Haven: Yale University Press.

D. Smith-Christopher (2002), *A Biblical Theology of Exile*, Overtures to Biblical Theology; Minneapolis: Fortress Press.

R. S. Sugirtharajah (ed.) (1991), *Voices from the Margin: Interpreting the Bible in the Third World*, Maryknoll: Orbis.

C. C. Torrey (1910), *Ezra Studies*, reprinted 1970, New York: KTAV.

V. Westhelle (2008), 'Margins Exposed: Representation, Hybridity and Transfiguration', in R. S. Sugirtharajah (ed.) *Still at the Margins: Biblical Scholarship Fifteen Years after the Voices from the Margin*, London: T&T Clark, pp. 69–87.

8

EDWARD SAID'S *ORIENTALISM* AND THE MAKING OF A CONTRAPUNTAL HERMENEUTICS

R. S. Sugirtharajah

Edward Said 'reads the world as closely as he reads books'.

Salman Rushdie (1992, p. 166)

Orhan Pamuk's novel, *The New Life* (1998), begins with the bold claim of the narrator, Osman, 'I read a book one day and my whole life was changed.' Osman first came across the book in the hands of an attractive college girl called Janan, and bought a copy of it at a sidewalk stall on his way home. The book, whose contents are never fully disclosed but only alluded to, changes Osman's life so radically that he comes to believe that it was 'written expressly' for him alone. Thereupon he embarks on a journey which takes him around several Turkish towns in clapped-out buses, a journey which is in fact an intellectual and spiritual odyssey.

Unlike the twenty-year-old hero in Pamuk's novel, who was confident enough to pinpoint one book which instantly changed his life, mine was not a sudden revelatory experience prompted by a single book. It took place slowly, imperceptibly, after dabbling in a series of books. The arrival at the 'one' book was at the end of a gradual process of reading which was also a sequence of steps in self- growth and self-discovery until I could settle upon a title and claim that this was it. Looking back, the book which has had the greatest impact on my intellectual career, my way of thinking and looking at the world, has been Edward Said's *Orientalism* (1978). The choice of Said's book does not mean that other books did not play a significant part in my life. There are several Tamil novels which I still go back to. The novels of Ashokamitran, Jayakanthan and Sujatha continue to inspire and enthral me. What is distinctive about Said's book is that it gave me a new impetus, new energy, new possibilities and, more specifically, a rigorous theoretical focus at a time when I was embroiled in an academic environment which considered the West as universal and measured the rest of the world against it and constantly found it wanting.

I was not lucky enough to see Said's book in the hands of a beautiful girl as Pamuk's Osman did his book. I came across mine accidentally in Hudson's in Birmingham – just in time, for the shop was to become the victim of several corporate take-overs, and is currently a designer-garment outlet. As I was idly browsing the shelves, by chance I spotted *Orientalism*. I had not heard of Said before. Disciplinary tribal loyalty was strong at that time and reading outside your discipline was seen as a treacherous act. Cross-border reading, like texting, had not yet caught the imagination. Depending on one's point of view, it was this very book that made Said either a distinguished or a disreputable figure. If *Orientalism* had been the only book Said had ever written, it would still have guaranteed him a secure and eminent place among the great intellectual thinkers of our time.

Edward Said: a very short history

A brief word about Edward Said. He was a Palestinian Christian who was born in Jerusalem in 1935. He and his family were made refugees in the 1947 Arab–Israeli conflict and moved to Cairo and Lebanon before leaving for the United

States. He studied at Princeton and then Harvard, where he got his Ph.D. He was hired by Columbia University in 1963 and remained there till his death in 2003. Said was a richly complex figure who combined the seemingly incompatible roles of an academic innovator and a political activist. He was the author of several influential books on literary and musical criticism. These include *Beginnings: Intention and Method* (1975), *Orientalism* (1978), *The World, The Text and the Critic* (1983), *Musical Elaborations* (1991), *Culture and Imperialism* (1993) – a follow-up to *Orientalism* – *Freud and the non-European* (2003), *Humanism and Democratic Criticism* (2004), and *On Late Style*, a posthumously published collection of essays on literature, art and music (2006). These books emphasized the interconnection between knowledge production and power, and the constant need to question and read against the received and accepted wisdom of the powerful. As a political activist championing the cause of the Palestinian people, Said authored several controversial books. These include *The Question of Palestine* (1980), *Covering Islam* (1982), *After the Last Sky* (1986), *The Politics of Dispossession* (1994), and *The End of the Peace Process* (2000). What was fascinating about his political books was that they were not only scathing about the Israelis but also and equally scornful about the Palestinian leadership.

His two books *Orientalism* and *Culture and Imperialism* were instrumental in forming a sub-discipline known variously as Empire Studies, Colonial Discourse or Postcolonial Studies. Although I have selected *Orientalism* as the book which had a great impact on my thinking, I shall refer to his other writings and, especially, his *Culture and Imperialism* which in a sense forms a companion volume to *Orientalism*.

Said's text and its context

Orientalism has to be situated in its rightful context. It appeared at a time which marked an important phase in the political and intellectual life of West Asia. The years 1978–89 witnessed, as Gilbert Achcar put it, 'three outstanding events' in the political and scholarly arenas. The first two were from the world of politics. One was the Iranian clerical revolution, which paved the way for the establishment of the Islamic Republic, and the other was the Islam-led Afghan protest against the Soviet occupation. The third event, unlike the other two, belonged to the world of intellectual history, namely, the publication of Said's *Orientalism*. These events were precipitated by, among other things, a disillusionment with Marxism, both in the Middle East and in the West. The Marxist and socialist ideals which fuelled the Arabic nationalism of the previous decades faced a counter-offence from religious figures in the Arab world. In the West, anti-Marxist retaliation came from those within Marxist circles who raised serious ideological questions about its utility. Said's book, published during this very period, further helped to dilute the efficacy of Marxian thinking. Said saw Marxism as a 'Romantic redemptive project' and Marx's economic analysis as 'a standard Orientalist undertaking, even though Marx's humanity, his sympathy for the misery of people, are clearly engaged' (Said 1978, p. 154). Said's contention was that in regard to current intellectual, political and cultural concerns, Marxism was more restrictive than enabling. This was rather surprising given that Said had acknowledged the influence on his work of Marxist authors such as Antonio Gramsci, Raymond Williams, Georg Lukács. Even those who were sympathetic to the central insight of *Orientalism* found Said's dismissal of Karl Marx a bit unjust.

What *Orientalism* most notably did was to expose three things: 1. the unholy alliance between colonialism and the European Enlightenment; 2. the complex relationship between Western culture and empire; and 3. Europe's need to invent the Orient for its own self-definition. If you stripped off the polemics, controversy and argument, *Orientalism* was simply about authenticity and integrity. Phrased differently, the book raised questions about representation: 'How does one *represent* other cultures? What is *another* culture? Is the notion of a distinct culture (or race, religion, civilization) a useful one, or does it always get involved either in self-congratulation (when one discusses one's own) or hostility and aggression (when one discusses the 'other')? How do ideas acquire authority, 'normality', and even the status of 'natural' truth (Said 1978, pp. 325–6)?

Said was not the first to examine the troubled relationship between the West and the East. How the West portrayed non-Western peoples had been addressed before. There were other thinkers and writers both in the East and in the West who had studied the uneasy association between the Occident and the Orient. There were Arabist and Islamic scholars such as A. L. Tibawi, Syed Hussein Alatas, Anouar Abdel-Malek, Hichem Djait, Indian writers such as K. M. Panikkar, K. Ananda Coomaraswamy, and Far-Eastern thinkers like Tenshin Okakura, who highlighted the unfair and the highly opinionated rendering of the Orient by the Occident. Said not only amplified and extended their work, but also added several new critical dimensions. First, to the reports of colonial administrators, anthropologists, geographers and travellers, Said added another category – literary writings. He was thus able to expose the colonial assumptions and empire values embedded in the novels of Jane Austen and Rudyard Kipling. His contention was that these literary works endorsed the values and morals of the empire rather than commenting critically upon them. But Said was quick to add that the validation of the empire in the writings of these distinguished literary figures did not in any way diminish the value or the talent of these writers. What he encouraged was not a dismissal of these texts, not an outright rejection of them for their tainted or distorted views, but a re-reading and re-examining of them. I will address the issue of his using these Western writings again, in the latter part of this piece. Second, his work combined a number of instruments – historical scholarship, literary and rhetorical analysis, and theories of the relationship between power and knowledge. Third, where Said differed from earlier exponents was in his ability to assemble assorted and isolated fields such as 1. Islamic Studies, Indic Studies, Philology, 2. critical concepts such as Romanticism and Enlightenment; and 3. the liberative thrust of Third-World oppressed groups. He amalgamated these into an accomplished but at the same time an argumentative discourse called Orientalism. Whereas the earlier attempts were undertaken within the preserve of a single discipline, Said's work transcended disciplinary boundaries and sought connections across a variety of disciplines. At the same time, he urged other scholars to see the larger picture and not to be tied to particular specialisms which tend to shut out other fields such as art, politics and history.

What was disturbing about Said's work was that instead of locking up these findings in the safe confines of the academy, he unleashed them into the world at large, thus simultaneously challenging scholarly neutrality and making truth, freedom and representation major forces of academic writing. *Orientalism* was a timely warning about the limitations and the tainted nature of what passed for serious scholarship, and exposed the West's so-called objectivity as hostile and damaging to the people of the 'Orient'. It also called into question not only 'the possibility of nonpolitical scholarship but also the advisability of too close a relationship between the scholar and the state' (Said 1978, p. 326). Put at its simplest, Said expected scholarship to be not only erudite but also ethical and committed to serving the dominated rather than the dominant.

Said's *Orientalism* was by no means an immaculate book. It had a number of flaws which Said himself went on to rectify in the various introductions and afterwords that he wrote for subsequent editions and also in his other writings, especially his *Culture and Imperialism* and *Humanism and Democratic Criticism*. He was gracious enough to concede James Clifford's criticism that *Orientalism* relapses 'into the essentializing mode it attacks'. His *Culture and Imperialism* highlighted examples of indigenous resistance to colonialism which hardly got a mention in *Orientalism*. While recording the literary and ideological achievements of these dissenting voices, Said, at the same time, did not shy away from exposing the excessive nationalism entrenched in some of the anti-colonial liberation movements. Some critics found his methods self-contradictory. He was accused of employing the values of the Enlightenment to attack the very culture that produced it. There is another tension that runs in his writing. While attacking cultural conservatism, his cultural interests were blatantly elitist and traditional. One area where he failed miserably was in appreciating popular culture and incorporating it into his interpretative framework.

He was a great devotee of opera and classical music and was himself a notable pianist. His valedictory collection of essays, *On Late Style*, was a paean to Western canonical writers and high-culture artists. He found himself accused concurrently of being anti-West by right-wing commentators and pro-West by nationalists. Although it was not a fault of his own, Said was blamed for giving comfort to fundamentalists who erroneously used his works for their anti-West bashing. A simplistic reading of Said by these fundamentalists resulted in the rhetoric of blame without grasping Said's complex balancing of the intertwined and overlapping historical experiences of the invader and the invaded.

A popular misperception of *Orientalism* is that it is anti-Western and anti-missionary and that it is all about the nastiness of the empire. But Said makes it clear that the empire was not always about cruelty and vengeance. He readily acknowledges the enormous contribution of European scholars in the fields of Indic, Arabic and Chinese studies, and in how they unearthed manuscripts, revived vernacular languages, systematized grammar and studied the religious rituals of the people whom they ruled. In India, the discovery of past national glories and textual treasures aroused a national awakening which, in an ironic way, led to an anti-Western resistance and the eventual collapse of the Western empires. All these Said does not dispute. In fact, he salutes the pioneering and painstaking efforts of the earlier Orientalists. Said's contention, however, is that an enlightened study of other cultures was limited to a small group of interested and progressive Europeans. His concern was with some of the negative signals that emanated from such study, and the purposes to which it was put. What these scholarly enterprises did was to generalize, essentialize and fix the cultures of the colonized. As Said put it:

> As a system of thought about the Orient, it always rose from the specifically human detail to the general transhuman one; an observation about a tenth-century Arab poet multiplied itself into a policy towards (and about) the Oriental mentality in Egypt, Iraq or Arabia. Similarly a verse from the Koran would be considered the best evidence of an ineradi-

cable Muslim sensuality. Orientalism assumed an unchanging Orient absolutely different from the West. (Said 1978, p. 96)

His problem with Oriental studies, as he explained in one of his 'Afterwords', was with a small guild of Orientalists who had 'a specific history of complicity with the imperial power, which it would be Panglossian to call irrelevant'. His contention was that 'we are still required to ask where, how and with what supporting institutions and agencies such studies take place *today?*' (Said 2003, p. 342).

After Said's *Orientalism*, which looked in detail at such topics as construction of colonial knowledge, the reification of racial and religious stereotypes, and organizational practices of the state, it is almost impossible to read any literary work, including the Bible and its interpretation, without being alert to the presence of the empire, colonialism and imperial intentions.

For the discipline in which I work – biblical studies – time came to a halt in the nineteenth century. In my earlier years in the discipline, some scholars were like the Japanese soldiers coming out of the Philippine jungles not realizing that time had moved on and that the war was long over. Mainstream biblical scholarship was still in awe of the German historical-critical method. It was engaged in research into such momentous issues as the number of times Paul had used the active participle in his epistles. Biblical studies was, on the whole, entrenched in such endless and pointless exercises. It was at that time mind-numbingly abstract and tediously technical and had nothing to do with what was going on in life. Liberation hermeneutics, which was trying to see connections between the text and the context, was dismissed in a characteristically patronizing tone as 'interesting but not proper exegesis'. The reigning biblical scholarship was too local and too Eurocentric but pretended to be universal. It was at this juncture that Said's book came as a sense of relief to people like me who were floundering in our hermeneutical journey under heavy toxic doses of Western theories and ideas. It was Said's book which brought me out of this comatose state and provided the tools to interrogate the text, the world and our place in it. Said's book not only provided a relief in my inchoate hermeneutical frustrations but also matched them with compelling tuition on how to approach a text and fashion new questions.

Tips, hints and pointers

At this juncture, Said's book came as a great relief and illuminated my academic life. It provided me with a number of tips, hints and pointers. One of the tips I got from Said was how to interrogate a text and ask questions such as: What does a narrative include? What does it exclude? In an interview, Said said that he had always been interested in what gets left out: 'I'm interested in the tension between what is represented and what isn't represented, between the articulate and the silent' (Bayoumi and Rubin 2000, p. 424). It was Said who made me aware of 'the possibilities for the interpreter to bring out voices which, to the author or to the composer, may not have been apparent' (Bayoumi and Rubin 2000, p. 425). It was with Said's encouragement that I was able to situate empire at the centre of the Bible, and ask about the neglected imperial dimensions and undertones and the allusive silences embedded in the text. While mainstream studies were concerned with historical, theological and spiritual aspects of the Bible, I was able to add the often overlooked issue of the politics of empire and the ideological nature of interpretation. In doing so, I was able to pose questions such as: How does the author portray the empire – as compassionate, or repressive? Does the text strengthen the imperial cause or destabilize it? Where does the allegiance of the author lie – with those in power or those made powerless by colonial occupation? How does the author represent the occupied – as thankful recipients or as hapless victims? Does the author provide space for their resistance?

The second important lesson I learnt from Said was that 'each cultural work is a vision of a moment, and we must juxtapose that vision with various revisions it later provoked' (Said 1993, p. 79). This meant what he calls reading texts contrapuntally. It was from Said that I got the idea about contrapuntal reading – a model of reading practice which I found useful for my work. He utilizes the compositional analogy known as counter-point from the world of music:

> In the counterpoint of Western classical music, various themes play off one another, with only a provisional privilege being given to any particular one; yet in the resulting polyphony there is a concert and order, and an organized interplay that derives from the themes and not from a rigorous melodic or formal principle outside the work. (Said 1993, pp. 59–60)

Said explained the contrapuntal method thus: 'The point is that the contrapuntal reading must take account of both processes, that of imperialism and that of resistance to it, which can be done by extending our reading of the texts to include what was once forcibly excluded' (Said 1993, p. 79). For him, contra-puntal reading was not the same as the old comparative litera-ture model but an 'atonal ensemble' which 'takes into account all sorts of spatial or geographical and rhetorical practices – inflections, limits, constraints, intrusions, inclusions, prohibi-tions – all of them tending to elucidate a complex and uneven topography' (Said 1993, p. 386). As Said put it, a contrapuntal reading is one in which 'Dickens and Thackeray as London authors are read also as writers whose historical influence is informed by the colonial enterprises in India and Australia of which they were so aware, and in which the literature of one commonwealth is involved in the literatures of others' (Said 1993, pp. 385–6). In such a model of reading, one can admire the works of Austen and Kipling as literature even if their texts are peppered with colonial intentions and Eurocentric views. Elsewhere in my writings, I have explained and given examples of how I have used this method profitably for biblical studies.

The third hint I got from Said was that marginality and migrancy are not to be trumpeted eternally but have to be brought to a close. When some of those engaged in marginal hermeneutics and identity politics asserted their status of mar-ginality itself as a sign of divine election, and claimed that such a special status gave them an exclusive access to truth, Said warned against any such inflated privileges. For him, they were only stepping stones and not stabilized zones to be settled in permanently. He warned against the marginal voices repeating the sins of the dominant hermeneutics, 'becoming institutionalized, marginality turning into separatism, and resistance hardening into dogma' (Said 1993, p. 63). He emphasized the need to be self-critical and vigilant. The lesson for these marginal interpreters is not to lionize their traditions or claim divine sanction for their cause as some Dalits and women seem to do, but to read and investigate their resources inquiringly, sceptically and searchingly, with proper rigour. To make marginal causes the only serviceable interpretative task will not only restrict our vision but also arrest our growth and prevent us from participating, intervening and contributing to issues which affect the whole of humanity.

Resistance, relevance

Looking back now at what Said wrote three decades ago, *Orientalism* may not look stunningly original or daring today. Partly this is due to the fact that so many of its insights have been incorporated into the mainstream, or better nuanced by those who followed Said and, in some cases, have been overtaken by new contemporary concerns. The old territorial colonialism which provided the backdrop for Oriental scholarship is almost over. The modern colonialism takes different forms and requires new tools and new texts in order to challenge it. The Orient itself, which the West refashioned in its own image, has undergone momentous changes. There is a new verve and vibrancy in India and China. The cultural and political landscape of the Middle East too has been altered drastically. Nonetheless, the issues Said raised in that book still remain valid.

Surely, the most enduring legacy of *Orientalism* has been to make scholars aware that their work has political undertones, implications and repercussions whether they had intended it or not. Said wanted to expose as bogus the claim of scholarship to be ideologically neutral. This does not mean that facts do not count any more or evidence does not have any value. What in effect Said was asking for was to substitute the worn-out dogmas of neutrality and balance with the criterion of fairness. What this means is that scholars ought to be conscious of the sources they deal with and the controlling institutional circumstance out of which their knowledge is produced and circulated. They need to be aware of how they employ sources, against whom and on whose behalf these sources are put to use. What in effect the book did was to help make scholars more conscious of their own presuppositions, privileges and responsibilities. More vitally, they should be attentive to the fact that their scholarly works can be adapted and reshaped by political leaders, lobbyists and syndicated columnists to strengthen the ideological hold of the powerful and to provide information to authorities like multinational corporations and financial institutions who wield power over people.

Said's persistent call for criticism to be oppositional still remains pertinent. For Said, criticism and opposition are like conjoined twins. They are inseparable. The chief responsibility of criticism is to be 'constitutively opposed to every form of tyranny, domination and abuse', with, as its 'social goals', production of 'non-coercive knowledge' for life enhancement and human freedom. The significance of criticism lies in its refusal to be neutered. For Said, criticism is essentially an 'instrument of intervention' which helps to unveil the struggles of the oppressed and also exposes the lies of the oppressor. What Said advocated as the central aspect of a critic's life – 'a critical attitude and maintaining a critical position' – is still a worthy principle to be upheld and emulated.

Said's call to the intellectuals to recover the old amateur spirit is another virtuous trait that is worth upholding. The current emphasis on management-led research, or, as Terry Eagleton put it, 'managerialization of mind', has resulted in restricting the area of knowledge and has helped to increase what Said calls 'technical formalism'. Specialization is seen as a prerequisite for a career and creates 'the cult of the certified expert'. What Said encouraged was scholarship which was disinterested in rewards and certification by proper authorities and driven by 'care and affection'. This is an apt message for biblical studies that is so entrenched in bias and pretentious methods and techniques, whose sole aim is self-preservation of those who practice it.

This is probably the right place to get back to the issue of how to handle Western texts – an issue I referred to earlier. At a time when texts are being ruthlessly purified of their gender and racial biases, and canonical works are being mindlessly rejected, Said's sane advice is well worth adhering to. For him, what ultimately mattered was not

> *who* wrote what, but rather *how* a work is written and *how* it is read. The idea that because Plato and Aristotle are male and products of a slave society they should be disqualified from receiving contemporary attention is as limited an idea as suggesting that *only* their work, because it was addressed to and about elites, should be read today. (Said 2000, p. 385)

Said wanted to move away from the tedious debate between those who advocated the superiority of Western classics and those who championed the purity of native literature. He cautioned against those who wanted to exclude the talents of literary figures simply because their work was tainted by being undertaken at the height of imperialism. His stance was that

> we must therefore read the great canonical texts, and perhaps also the entire archive of modern and pre-modern European and American culture, with an effort to draw out, extend, give emphasis and voice to what is silent or marginally present or ideologically represented in such works. (Said 1993, p. 78)

What he advocated was a balancing of the literature of the empire with anti-imperialist writing. For him, the critical issue was about 'interdependence between things' and seeing the 'connection between things' (Said 1993, p. 408). Said repeatedly made it clear that it was 'possible to articulate them *together*, as an ensemble, as having a relationship that is more than coincidental, conjectural, mechanical' (1993, p. 58). He echoes the Fanonian idea of binding 'the European as well as the native together in a new non-adversarial community of awareness and anti-imperialism' (Said 1993, p. 331).

Said's relentless resistance to forcing 'cultures and peoples into separate and distinct breeds or essences' is still relevant at a time when nations, religions and cultures are trying to forge a monolithic story. In his writings, he maintains that no nation, culture, ideology or religious tradition was a model of virtue or of vice. Linked to this was his other persistent theme, that there was no such thing as a pure and isolated culture. Such a view leads to 'territorially reductive polarizations' such as 'us' and 'them', 'the West' and 'Islam'. For him, all cultures and religions were a mixture of good and evil, of truth and untruth, freedom and suppression. The only way to make one's nation, culture or religion less fanatical and exclusive was to broaden it by critical mixing and borrowing from one another. This is a slow process and it needs time, persistence, critical awareness and sophistication.

Finally, Said's advocacy for humanism still continues to be relevant. In spite of the contemptuous dismissal of the word, Said continued to speak relentlessly of the benefits of humanism. For him, it is a rational, secular and communitarian-based hermeneutical tool, and specifically a useful weapon against national and religious orthodoxies. It is, in his view, the 'only' and the 'final resistance we have against the inhuman practices and injustices that disfigure human history' (Said 2003, p. xxii). Said defines humanism thus:

> By humanism I mean first of all attempting to dissolve Blake's mind-forg'd manacles so as to be able to use one's mind historically and rationally for the purpose of reflective understanding and genuine disclosure. Moreover, humanism is sustained by a sense of community with other interpreters and other societies and periods: strictly speaking, therefore, there is no such thing as an isolated humanist. (Said 2003, p. xvii)

Said's understanding of humanism is not the traditional, exclusive European one which aims to protect and trumpet European values, but one more attuned 'to the non-European, genderized, decolonized, and decentered energies and currents of our time' (Said 2004, p. 47). Said questions the notion that humanism is a pure product of the West. He refers its origins to

Islamic textual practices, locates it in the medieval Muslim universities and he acknowledges contributions of Indian, Chinese, Japanese and African cultures which have all been 'laundered clean of that heterogeneity so troublesome to current humanism' (Said 2004, p. 54). The humanism he advocates is 'an unsettling adventure in difference, in alternative traditions, in texts that need a new deciphering within a much wider context' (Said 2004, p. 55).

At a time when it was unfashionable to talk about meta-stories, Said spoke insistently of the need for some of them. He kept on reminding us that emancipation and reconciliation were great ideas and themes that still had powerful purchase. Taking issue with Lyotard's announcement of the death of grand narratives, Said wrote that these 'grand narratives remain, even though their implementation and realization are at present in abeyance, deferred, or circumvented' (Said 2003, p. 351). Meta-narratives may be over for the West, but for the politically, economically and sexually marginalized, emancipation still remains a potential to be realized. Similarly, reconciliation as a grand narrative among warring groups of people is an unrealized possibility. He was advocating reconciliation between the colonized and the colonizer, as he did between Israelis and Palestinians, without reducing histories, identities and cultures.

To conclude: the relationship between the book and the reader is not one-sided, as it is often portrayed and presumed to be. Actually, it is a mutual exchange. A book allures and transforms the reader, and at the same time and in large measure, its meaning changes. Neither the book nor the reader remains static. It was one of the Greek philosophers who observed that no one crosses the same river twice. The river is different and the one who wishes to cross it is also different. On looking back, both I and *Orientalism* have changed over the years. We are neither of us the same. I began with the epiphany of Pamuk's hero Osman. Let me end with his thought about this curious transubstantiation that takes place between the reader and the book: 'So it was that as I read my point of view was transformed by the book, and the book was transformed by my point of view' (Pamuk 1998, p. 60).

References

M. Bayoumi and A. Rubin (2000), *The Edward Said Reader*, London: Granta Books.

O. Pamuk (1998), *The New Life*, London: Faber & Faber.

S. Rushdie (1992), *Imaginary Homelands: Essays and Criticism 1981–1991*, London: Granta Books.

E. W. Said (1978), *Orientalism*, London: Penguin Books.

E. W. Said (1993), *Culture and Imperialism*, London: Chatto & Windus.

E. W. Said (2000), *Reflections on Exile and Other Essays*, Cambridge Mass.: Harvard University Press.

E. W. Said (2003), *Orientalism*, London: Penguin Books.

E. W. Said (2004), *Humanism and Democratic Criticism*, New York: Columbia University Press.

Part Two

SENSE AND SENSITIVITY: THEOLOGICAL TEXTS

9

READING GUTIÉRREZ
AMONG THE 'PANDAS'

Kwok Pui-lan

Gustavo Gutiérrez's book *A Theology of Liberation* was published in time to save me from the 'pandas' in my college days. 'Panda' was a nickname we had given to the radical, left-leaning students in Hong Kong, who wore dark blue, high-collared Mao jackets in the winter, slung a misty green canvas bag on their shoulders, and wore round plastic eyeglasses. They could be easily mistaken for comrades from Chinese central casting. They were called 'pandas' because the Chinese for pandas consists of two characters, which mean 'bear-cat', and the character 'bear' is a homonym for 'red' in Cantonese, such that the words may mean 'pandas' or 'red cats'.

I was not one of the 'pandas'. My feelings toward them oscillated between ambivalence on a good day to cynicism when I was in a bad mood. On the one hand, I admired their youthful idealism and their romantic dream of turning the world upside down. They were the students who camped out at the Student Union, created placards for demonstrations, and encouraged students to 'know about the fatherland and be concerned about society' – the slogan of the student movement in those days. As many of us were the first in our family to attend college and had come from working-class families, I admired the self-sacrifice of the 'pandas' and their commitment to a noble cause. The president of the Student Union, for example, went on to become a factory worker after graduation, to organize the labour movement, instead of leading a more comfortable life as a colonial official or a high-school teacher. On the other hand, these 'pandas' could be self-righteous and arrogant, presuming that they were more socially conscientized than others and intolerant of other views. They were so 'red', and their hearts so turned to Communist China, that they could hardly see anything wrong with her. Since they were die-hard atheists, they dismissed those of us who were studying theology as wasting our time, if not trapped in our false consciousness. I recall that a theological student in the Masters' programme who had graduated from a Taiwanese university was so appalled by them that he decided to go to the Student Union to debate with the 'red cats'. To our relief, the encounter ended only in fiery words, but not in blood.

A Theology of Liberation was translated into English in 1973 and was widely read among my peers at the time. Gutiérrez appealed to me, because his concern with social justice was palpable in the text, a concern also shared by the 'pandas'. Yet, unlike these 'pandas', Gutiérrez did not think pursuing justice and working for social transformation as antithetical to Christianity. On the contrary, such actions lie at the very heart of theology and Christian mission. Theology without action is dead, he said, pure and simple. His book helped me to see the vocation of a theologian, even though the colonial situation in Hong Kong was very different from the dire poverty of his native country Peru or the wider Latin American society, which he was addressing. Gutiérrez's image of Jesus as the liberator fired one up and motivated one into action much faster than Tillich's abstract Christ as the New Being or Barth's distant God as the Wholly Other. After reading these great European theologians, one had a sense that they were scratching the itchy foot without first taking off the boot, as the Chinese would say. In short, they had not touched the crux of the matter.

While in college, I had the privilege of joining a small travel seminar organized by the Student Christian Movement, which brought us to Japan, Korea and the Philippines. I remember talking with progressive students at the University of Philippines who told us that they (women and men) took turns going to prison to fight against the Marcos dictatorship. In Seoul, the

Park Chung Hee government was so repressive that we had to change our meeting places occasionally for fear that we were being followed or wiretapped. In the midst of the beauty and serenity of the shrines of Kyoto, we heard the peace movement that Japanese Christians had initiated and their determination to repent for the crimes perpetuated by their government during World War Two. These Asian Christian leaders were involved in the struggle for democracy, human rights, demilitarization and economic justice, problems that beset many newly independent countries. During the trip, my heart felt very heavy when I saw first-hand the suffering faces of the Asian people, but I also glimpsed what Bonhoeffer had said about the cost of discipleship and the grace of God.

In the 1970s, Asian theologians became more interested in the contextualization of theology, with its focus on sociopolitical issues, than in indigenization, which was concerned primarily with recasting the Christian message in Asian cultures and idioms. The World Conference on Mission and Evangelism, held in Bangkok in 1973 with the theme 'Salvation Today', highlighted a holistic salvation, and not just the salvation of souls. The participants from Hong Kong brought back the message that salvation concerned the whole person and the whole community, since the body and the soul could not be separated. This soon spurred the debate whether the churches should focus on propagating the gospel or on social concerns, as most of the churches in Hong Kong were evangelical to the core. Looking back, the harsh criticism of the 'pandas' might have had a point, since many evangelical students on campus thought that Christian mission should focus on the former and not the latter, as if the two could be separated. I found Gutiérrez's insistence of the Church's 'preferential option for the poor' helpful not only in deflecting criticism from the 'red cats' on the left, but also in struggling with the 'holier than thou cats' on the right.

I had not travelled in China, except to my parents' native villages, until my honeymoon in the late 1970s. Travel in China was not easy in those days, and people in Hong Kong, half of whom were refugees from China, were generally afraid of the Communist regime. As my husband and I rowed a boat in Hangzhou's peaceful West Lake and strolled down the tree-lined streets of Nanjing, we were infused with the beauty of our 'homeland', from which Hong Kong had been separated since the defeat of the 1842 Opium War. Yet, we were keenly aware of the material poverty and the low standard of living. For example, when we went to the shops selling fruit and beverages, we would ask for the red and succulent oranges or apples inside the glass counters, instead of the dry and blemished ones found in the baskets. The comrades behind the counter would tell us in a terse voice, and sometimes with indignation, that these better apples or oranges were not for sale. They were lining the counters for decoration, I supposed.

I remember very vividly one evening when we had gone to the Hanshan Temple in Suzhou because a well-known poet had written about the tolls of its bell, and we had missed our dinner at our hotel. We thought that we could buy something to eat from the shops that were still open. To our surprise, we could not buy any rice, noodles or cakes because basic staples and meat were rationed and unavailable without coupons. We overseas Chinese and foreigners had to eat at our hotels or other designated places. We were very hungry and hopped from shop to shop, until an elderly man took pity on us and sold us two pieces of cake for the night. We were shocked that money could not open doors, which would have seemed unbelievable in capitalist Hong Kong. Yet, we were impressed by an economic system that put people's basic needs first, instead of setting its goals on making profits and earning much-needed foreign currency.

I had a chance to engage more deeply with Marxist social analysis when I wrote my Master's thesis comparing power and justice in Mao Zedong's thought with Reinhold Niebuhr's ethics. As Gutiérrez had drawn insights from Marxist social theory, I wanted to find out what Mao's thought had to offer to contemporary social ethics. While Mao was trying to adapt Marxist analysis to a dirt-poor China, Niebuhr was writing his important work *Moral Man and Immoral Society* (1932). Niebuhr argued that the moral ideals of love and self-sacrifice are more applicable to individuals in personal relationships, but are less workable in collectives, such as the nation, which can only strive for justice through a balance of power. Mao would not agree, for he had wanted to create a 'reign of virtue' in China – he intended not only to revolutionize China's social structures, but also people's consciousness through the Cultural Revolution (1966–76). Mao would think Niebuhr's Christian realism had not gone far enough, and that the lofty ideals of democracy and balance of power have proven time and again to serve only bourgeois interests. Niebuhr's ethics and political philosophy would have sounded too timid, too calculated to Mao's ears. Mao had famously said:

> A revolution is not a dinner party, or writing an essay, or painting a picture, or doing embroidery; it cannot be so refined, so leisurely and gentle, so temperate, kind, courteous, restrained and magnanimous. A revolution is an insurrection, an act of violence by which one class overthrows another.

The Chinese revolution had inspired a generation of anti-colonial revolutionary leaders, from Frantz Fanon in Algeria to Ho Chih Minh in Vietnam. They had looked to China as a shining example for the Third World and an alternative to the exploitative capitalist system. In the 1960s and 1970s, some of the leaders of the New Left in the United States and Europe had romanticized China to such an extent that they might have thought that the Kingdom of God had descended from heaven with Beijing as the capital. I wondered if Latin American theologians had also been intrigued by China, or if they had looked closer to home to the Cuban revolution for inspiration. If José Miguez Bonino had written a volume on *Doing Theology in a Revolutionary Situation* (1975), he and his colleagues would certainly be interested in what a 'post-revolutionary' situation would look like.

To a certain extent, China at that time could boast that she had put into practice what Gutiérrez had written about the preferential option for the poor – private property was eradicated, land and modes of production became collectively owned, preferential treatment was given to peasants and workers who were formerly oppressed, girls received education and women had work. Yet the Communist regime had restricted the freedom of speech and organization, put dissidents in jail, violated human rights, caused family members to betray one another, and inflicted pain and suffering on intellectuals on a scale unprecedented in Chinese history. With Mao's death in 1976 and the downfall of the Gang of Four, the naked power-struggle within the Communist Party and the havoc this had wreaked on the whole nation could no longer be concealed. Sadly, the Red Guards had not brought the Kingdom of God to China, but purgatory. Unlike Niebuhr and Gutiérrez, the Chinese leaders did not seem to have a serious grasp of the human propensity to sinfulness and therefore had not developed a political system to hold power abuse at bay. Even with phenomenal economic development in China in the past decades, democracy to this day remains a very distant dream.

In 1984, I went to Harvard to begin my doctoral studies, and I was exposed to a wider range of responses to and assessments of Latin American liberation theology. Not long after I arrived in Cambridge, Massachusetts, the bookstores around Harvard were putting Leonardo Boff's book *Church, Charism, and Power* (1986) on prominent display. The Brazilian theologian was silenced by the Vatican because he dared to apply Marxist class analysis to the study of the hierarchical Roman Catholic Church. Needless to say, this controversy made his book an instant bestseller, and my professor at Harvard, Harvey Cox, later wrote a book, *The Silencing of Leonardo Boff* (1988), in response. Although the Congregation for the Doctrine of the Faith has affirmed the widening gap between the rich and the poor and the yearning for social justice, its instructions on the theology of liberation have condemned its Marxist approach and especially what has been perceived as the reduction of sin to its social level.

I had become aware that Marxism was a hot-button word in American academia. Marxism could create a knee-jerk reaction among the students even though they might not have studied it. For many faculty and students in the liberal US divinity schools, theology largely means a rational pursuit of knowledge of God, and not 'critical reflection on praxis' as Gutiérrez has described. While progressive faculty and students at Harvard at the time were protesting against apartheid in South Africa, I did not see a concomitant fervour to eradicate racism and classism in their own backyard. Harvard, as the richest private university in the world, colluded with the interests of the ruling class in many ways. This meant that I had to plan a study programme that would be self-directed and self-motivated and that served my own needs. Instead of taking the usual courses, I had taken many independent study courses, which allowed me to read feminist theology, critical theory, and Chinese history and literary writings, and to attend luncheon talks and public lectures offered within or near the university. I was very fortunate to have studied with Benjamin I. Schwartz on China in this way and listened to Alice Walker, Jacques Derrida, Maxine Hong Kingston, Mercy Amba Oduyoye, Robert McAfee Brown, Juan Luis Segundo, Sallie McFague, and so forth when they visited Boston.

I did not have a female professor when I was studying theology in Hong Kong, though I have had the privilege of learning from some of the leading feminist theologians teaching in the Boston area. Not surprisingly, many of the pioneers in feminist theology in the US have been Roman Catholic because their Church had barred women from ordination and still refuses to recognize the full ministry of women. Mary Daly's first book published in 1968 was entitled *The Church and the Second Sex*. I was interested in the commonalities and differences between feminist liberation theology that emerged during the second-wave women's movement in the US and Latin American liberation theology.

The work of Elisabeth Schüssler Fiorenza is particularly important for her critique of the model of biblical interpretation in Latin American theology, especially the hermeneutical circle proposed by Juan Luis Segundo, a leading theologian from Uruguay. In *Bread Not Stone* (1984), Schüssler Fiorenza challenges Segundo for failing to bring a critical evaluation to bear upon the biblical texts and upon the process of interpretation. Thus, Segundo's interpretation is more a 'hermeneutics of consent', which does not question biblical contents, especially those traditions that evidently marginalize women or have the potential to do so. While reading *A Theology of Liberation*, I had the hunch that Gutiérrez had found the Bible to be a friend and ally, because the prophets and Jesus had spoken on behalf of the poor. He and other male liberation theologians have not provided adequate guidelines to deal with those parts of the Bible that are oppressive to women. This observation led me to look at some of the pioneering works in Asian theology anew, as some of the authors had also failed to question the androcentric language and sexist ideologies found in the Bible.

While studying in the US, I had the privilege of getting to know some of the pioneers in womanist theology, *mujerista* theology, Latina theology, and Asian American feminist theology. It was a very exciting period because we were all searching for our voices, rediscovering our heritages, and articulating new theological models. Because racial and ethnic minority women experience multiple oppressions, we know that a theology that focuses on class, gender or race alone would not be adequate for our salvation. Our biblical interpretation and theology must follow a multi-axle framework, for the different forms of oppression intersect with each other and cannot be separated. As womanist theologian Delores Williams reminds us, while white women have criticized patriarchy, they have often forgotten that the same white patriarchal institutions that they have criticized – the police, nation-state and businesses – have offered them protection and privileges, which are often denied to people of colour.

Since people knew that I had come from Hong Kong, I was invited to speak about women in China and the status of women in a socialist country. I have talked about women and work in China and business ethics from a Chinese feminist perspective in professional gatherings. For the majority of the US feminist theologians, class and economic justice are not their priority concerns, as most of their works focus on gender and sexuality issues. A notable exception is Beverly Wildung Harrison, a Christian feminist social ethicist who has written on abortion as well as economic exploitation. I had the privilege of staying in her apartment in New York after I had defended my dissertation and was waiting for my commencement. She had worked with Reinhold Niebuhr and offered a very astute feminist critique of his work.

After graduation, I taught both in Hong Kong and the United States and used Gutiérrez's book in my courses. But I did not have a chance to speak to him until May 2000, although I had heard him speak some years back in an ecumenical event in Sweden. I was invited as a panellist for a symposium to honour him, when he received an honorary doctorate from Southern Methodist University in Dallas, Texas. During our time together, I took pictures with him and with other panellists in front of the chapel's lush green lawn, and he asked me to send copies to him afterward. I took out my dog-eared copy of *A Theology of Liberation*, which had accompanied me across the Pacific several times, and asked him to sign it. On the front page, he carefully inscribed, 'To Pui Lan, In the same option, Gustavo Gutiérrez'. There was a book sale during the symposium and my book *Discovering the Bible in the Non-Biblical World* (1995) was on display. I asked Gutiérrez if he would like to have a copy of my book. To my surprise, he said that he had already read it, but he wanted to have a copy of his own. I bought a copy and autographed it for him. Then he said he should also buy a copy of one of his books and give it to me in return. I was amazed by his kind gesture and hastened to tell him, 'No, I can buy one and you can sign it for me.'

Gutiérrez is much shorter than I am, and I guess he might be less than five feet tall. He had suffered from a serious bout of osteomyelitis and stayed in bed for six years when he was a teenager. But he had a huge heart and a tenderness that I was privileged to witness that morning. We had a banquet with other honorees that evening, and Gutiérrez said he would go to the library to do some research that afternoon. He was still working so hard at 72, when most of us would have slowed or wound down. It was amazing to know that he still had the photographic memory and the agile mind that so many of his friends had admired.

I did not stay on to see Gutiérrez receive his honorary degree the next morning, for I had to fly back to Hong Kong after the symposium to visit my father who was very sick and dying. The trip to Hong Kong to visit family reminded me of my own roots and my theological beginning. The changes that had taken place in Hong Kong in the last quarter of a century were overwhelming and quite unbelievable. Instead of a British colony, Hong Kong has become a Special Administrative Region of the People's Republic of China since 1997. Although Hong Kong suffered from the Asian financial crisis in the late 1990s, she was poised to play instrumental roles in the economic development in China and compete with Shanghai as the key Chinese financial centre. The new Hong Kong airport that I saw for the first time boasted that it was one of the most modern and efficient in the world.

The 'pandas' could be found no more, either in Hong Kong or in China. Young people who were born after the Cultural Revolution probably could not believe that there was a time when a quarter of the world's population, women and men, wore the ubiquitous Mao jackets. College students in Hong Kong, as their counterparts elsewhere, are keener to earn money and climb the social ladder, than advocate for the poor and work for a social cause. Hong Kong has become so materialistic and absorbed into the neo-liberal market that it leaves little room for youthful idealism and students' political movements. If China had been a beacon of hope for the New Left, she may be an embarrassment or a nightmare now. When I visited Shenzhen, the Chinese city closest to Hong Kong, I could not believe the changes that had taken place, and no one would fully explain the complexities and contradictions of how this capitalist city could possibly exist in a so-called 'Communist' China.

Is liberation theology still relevant today, or has it run its course because its Marxist social analysis is outdated? After the disintegration of the former Soviet Union and the metamorphosis of China into a mixed economy, Marxist rhetoric seems to be so out of synch with the globalized market economy. If I were one of the 'pandas', I would have been so disillusioned by Marxism and, with it, liberation theology from Latin America. Fortunately, I have never joined the 'pandas' and have not put my entire hope either in capitalist development or in the dream of a classless society. I have seen the 'reign of virtue' in China and the devastation brought by the hero-worship of Mao. But as I have travelled more broadly and seen the great discrepancy between the lifestyles of the rich and the poor in the world, I have renewed interest in the question that Gutiérrez has put before us: How can we tell a poor and marginalized person that God loves him or her?

Since the 1990s, I have pursued this question not primarily through a Marxist framework, though I still think that a materialist analysis is important. Those of us who grew up after World War Two and lived through that period of scarcity would concur with Gutiérrez that poverty is a scandalous condition. But Marxist analysis has not provided much help in issues of gender and sexuality, and Karl Marx, just like his contemporaries, had a tendency to orientalize other societies. Thus, I have turned to postcolonial theories with a combination of critique of empire, cultural criticism, gender and Queer theory for help to look at the interlocking and multilayered oppression of societies long under colonialism. As the work of Gayatri Chakravorty Spivak has demonstrated, no one single theory is sufficient to analyse or bring solutions to the plight of the female subaltern. We have to continue to push the envelope and create spaces by opening the margins and seams of hegemonic theories and theologies.

My students sometimes ask me if I remain hopeful in this age of globalization and what roles the churches should play in it. I encourage them to think that there is globalization from above, which means the neo-liberal market, the World Bank, the International Monetary Fund, and the multinational corporations, but also globalization from below. Indian anthropologist Arjun Appradurai popularizes the idea of globalization from below or grassroots globalization. Grassroots globalization refers to the work of the nongovernmental organizations, the transnational advocacy networks, Amnesty International, public intellectuals, activists and socially concerned academics. Here faith communities will have definite roles to play, since many churches and denominations have established vast transnational networks across cultural and linguistic barriers.

I am aware that the cultural and political ethos of the Church is very different from the era following the Second Vatican Council, which has given impetus to the development of Latin American liberation theology. The Catholic Church has steadily placed more conservative bishops in Latin America, and with Pope Benedict XVI, the Church has become even more reactionary. In March 2007, the Congregation for the Doctrine of the Faith issued a statement saying that the work of Jon Sobrino is dangerous and erroneous. A leading Latin American theologian whose fellow Jesuits and house helpers were killed in 1989, Sobrino's work was criticized as placing too much emphasis on the humanity of Jesus. In the summer of the same year, the Vietnamese American theologian Peter C. Phan was also investigated because of his book *Being Religious Interreligiously* (2004). Phan has allegedly given a positive theological evaluation of non-Christian religion. Given that religious conflicts have fuelled much of the ethnic confrontations after the Cold War, the Vatican's position on other religions is backward looking and not conducive to interreligious understanding.

If we look beyond the Catholic Church, the future of global Christianity does not give us much optimism either. Christianity is going South, as Philip Jenkins has pointed out, for the majority of Christians will be living in the Southern hemisphere, practising a kind of Christianity that is more conservative and neo-orthodox. The conservative bishops from Asia and Africa, for example, have exerted far greater influences in the worldwide Anglican Communion, especially on the issue of homosexuality. The phenomenal growth of fundamentalist and Pentecostal churches is a force that mainline denominations have to reckon with. Given this conservative church climate, what is the future of liberative Christianity and what kinds of ecclesial movements are needed?

Just as we have to look at the globalization from below, we need to see the Church not from the centre, but from where the active movements of the people of God are taking place. At the turn of the millennium, churches from the North and the South were working on the Jubilee and the reduction of the tremendous burden of Third-World debt. I have colleagues and students who are working with the churches to promote the United Nations Millennium Development Goals, which aim to eradicate extreme poverty and hunger, combat HIV/AIDS and other diseases, provide universal primary education, and struggle for gender equality. There are grassroots networks, which link Christian women's movements in different parts of the world. The Internet and information technology have provided new opportunities for the exchange of information, activism, networking and collaboration.

I remain hopeful because I have seen changes in the churches and theology during my lifetime. When I first began to study theology, Mary Daly had not written her critical feminist work *Beyond God the Father* (1973), and women and racial minorities were just beginning to lift up their theological voices. Today, theology is no longer the prerogative of white men, as my students have not only Gutiérrez's work, but also the works of theologians of my generation to study and learn from. I anticipate that the next generation of theologians will have to address problems that we can barely imagine in our time. As Appradurai has said, globalization requires a new role for 'the imagination of social life'. Our next generation who grow up with instant messaging, iPods, iphones and Google will have to face the global issues of climate change, genetic engineering, arms race into space, massive migration, and acute poverty because traditional jobs have become redundant. If we have found the biblical metaphors of God as father, lord and warrior limiting, the next generation will be asked to imagine God in even more expansive and capacious ways.

They will have to come up with metaphors and images of a new heaven and a new earth that we could not have imagined. In giving birth to this new theology for the new millennium, I hope that my generation of theologians will be able to play a small part, just as Gutiérrez's generation has paved the way for us. As we celebrate his eightieth birthday in 2008, we offer thanks for his witness and for his abiding faith in the power of the poor in history.

References

L. Boff (1986), *Church, Charism and Power: Liberation Theology and the Institutional Church*, Maryknoll: Orbis.

J. M. Bonino (1975), *Doing Theology in a Revolutionary Situation*, Minneapolis: Fortress Press.

H. Cox (1988), *The Silencing of Leonardo Boff: The Vatican and the Future of World Christianity*, New York: Meyer, Stone & Co.

M. Daly (1973), *Beyond God the Father: Towards a Philosophy of Women's Liberation*, Boston: Beacon.

E. S. Fiorenza (1984), *Bread Not Stone: The Challenge of Feminist Biblical Interpretation*, Boston: Beacon.

G. Gutiérrez (1973), *A Theology of Liberation: History, Politics and Salvation*, Maryknoll: Orbis.

Kwok Pui-lan (1995), *Discovering the Bible in the Non-Biblical World*, Maryknoll: Orbis.

R. Niebuhr (1932), *Moral Man and Immoral Society: A Study in Ethics and Politics*, New York: Charles Scribner's Sons.

Peter C. Phan (2004), *Being Religious Interreligiously: Asian Perspectives on Interfaith Dialogue*, Maryknoll: Orbis.

10

READING *A THEOLOGY* *OF LIBERATION* FROM A *MUJERISTA* PERSPECTIVE

Ada María Isasi-Díaz

The flight from Caracas, Venezuela, to Lima, Peru, was not very long; at least, it did not seem very long to me. It was January 1967. After a short visit in Caracas with my parents and youngest sister, I had flown over the Andes and landed in Lima. I was being uprooted for the third time in six short years and was being planted in a radically different world from the one I knew. Barely ten days before, I had left the USA for the first time since arriving there from Cuba in September 1961. The trauma of arriving in the USA as a political refugee and the realization that I would not be able to return any time soon had impacted me greatly. I was 18 years old and with less than a month's notice I had to leave behind my whole world, the only world I knew: family, friends, country, societal mores and customs – from how to greet people to the appropriateness of public emotional display. Yes, I had been swiftly uprooted. Leaving Cuba became a defining event in my life.

Once in the USA, after a year in college, I entered the convent. This meant another radical uprooting for me. Back in the 1960s, those who entered the convent were remoulded, were made to fit into what the superiors thought was the way nuns should act and, yes, even how they should think. For two and a half years I did not see my family because they lived far from the novitiate or formation house. Communication with them was limited to my writing one letter a month and receiving letters from them once a week. Access to news about what was going on anywhere was limited to the headlines from the local newspaper that the superior chose to read to the community on Sundays. My years in the convent were fulfilling for I believed I was following my vocation, doing not only what I thought God wanted of me but also what I wanted to do with my life. This sense of accomplishment, however, was tempered by the loneliness and strangeness I felt, not only because I was in the convent, but because I was in the convent in a country and with a culture so different from my own.

I was in the convent for eight years. I wanted to stay for the rest of my life, but, alas, the superiors thought differently. Despite my difficulties with convent life I am most grateful for my time as a nun. It was a fruitful time for it helped me shape the desire to work with the poor that I had felt since I was a small girl. I will always be grateful, particularly for the fact that I was sent to work in Lima. I had the enormous good fortune and privilege of being there for three years during a very rich period in the life of the Church, a time marked by openness to change, to new possibilities, and to fresh perspectives.

The first half of the 1960s brought a great transformation to the Roman Catholic Church the world over. In 1959, shortly after being elected Pope, John XXIII had called a world council of all the bishops. He wanted, in his own words, to throw open the windows of the Church to be able to see out and allow the people to see in. Throwing open the windows, he said, would allow the Holy Spirit to renew the Church, to update the Church. *Aggiornamento*, Italian for 'update', became an everyday word in the Church. A year after I entered the convent, in the fall of 1962, the first session of the Second Vatican Council took place in Rome.

The changes introduced in the Church were profound ones. Many were immediately visible, for example, turning the altar so the priest faces the congregation instead of having his back to the people during Mass, using vernacular languages instead of Latin for the liturgy, a certain modicum of decentralization of authority that gave national bishops' conferences more say in shaping the Church, parish councils that made possible for the laity some participation in the governance of local churches, nuns shedding habits that belonged to past historical periods. All of these changes were rooted in deep theological shifts that modified the way in which the Roman Catholic Church has understood itself and its mission for centuries.

The Church in Lima was bubbling with change when I arrived there. Under the inspired leadership of Cardinal Landázuri Ricketts and with the help of a number of bishops, priests and nuns, the Church in Peru was moving boldly to embrace *aggiornamento* as fully as possible. I had entered the convent for the explicit purpose of being a missionary, so my superior assigned me to work in a poverty-stricken area of Lima where the nuns had a school for poor girls and a day-care centre for the babies and infants of the impoverished neighbourhood. When the Cardinal asked each congregation of nuns to appoint at least one of its members to work in the *Misión Conciliar*, an educational programme conducted in all the parishes of Peru to implement the changes ushered by Vatican II, the nun from my community chosen for this task became ill and I was her replacement. This made it possible for me to be much more than a teacher, to work in the parish where the school was located.

Among the priests I met during my three years in Lima was Gustavo Gutiérrez. One of my precious personal possessions is a mimeographed outline of 'theology of liberation' that he wrote and which I, among many others, discussed with students and laity in the parish. At that time what eventually came to be known as liberation theology was just beginning to be formulated. Its elaboration, I believe, drew inspiration from the commitment of many lay people, nuns and priests of the Church in Peru to bring about justice for those living in deplorable conditions.

Besides being deeply affected by the people among whom I worked, I was influenced by new understandings found in the documents of the Vatican Council regarding the nature and mission of the Church, the meaning of religious life, the purpose and shape of ministry, and the centrality of justice in the message of the gospel. Two books that circulated widely in the different groups in which I moved were also important in shaping my theological thinking as well as my personal life. The first one was a book written by Arturo Paoli, *La persona, el mundo, y Dios*. An Italian priest of the Congregation of the Little Brothers of Charles de Foucault living in Argentina, Paoli's commitment and message can be captured in two words, *justice* and *love* of the poor. These became the keystones of my own spirituality, of how I relate to God. Paoli's book helped me articulate my own vision of ministry and how I understand, even today, the kind of priorities and commitments that my religious faith demands of me. The other book was Paulo Freire's *Pedagogy of the Oppressed* (1970). Freire's work provided me with understandings that have influenced not only how I have carried out my ministry but also how I do theology. What I learned from my experiences among the destitute, my studies of Church documents, and my discussions of Paoli's and Freire's books helped me see that my work always has to contribute to creating societal conditions without which the poor and oppressed cannot become full agents of their own lives, remaining instead as passive objects of good intentions and charity. What I learned from these books, from the liberation theology movement that was emerging while I was in Lima, and from the way the destitute among whom I worked lived their faith, was the raw material from which I crafted my worldview, the lens through which, a few years later, I read Gutiérrez's book. It is the same lens I now use to re-read it.

By the time I bought and read for the first time Gustavo Gutiérrez's *A Theology of Liberation*, I had left the convent and was back in the USA. I read this book published in English in 1973 from my new 'location', in which I felt out of place – a way of feeling that has not changed much even today. My first reading of *A Theology of Liberation* filled me with joyful memories of my three years in Lima and helped me understand what I had experienced there. Three years had gone by since I left the convent, yet I was still in the midst of great personal turmoil. I was searching for a way to work on behalf of justice simply because to do so is life-giving to me. I knew that no matter what I did to earn a living, it had to be something that would allow me to work directly on confronting injustice. I have always needed my work to be a living of my religious faith that somehow challenges the Roman Catholic Church to open its windows to the ongoing work of the Spirit in our world, as John XXIII had wanted. My first reading of *A Theology of Liberation* was full of 'yes', and 'of course'. The underlining I did and the notes I jotted in the margins back then reveal that Gutiérrez's book provided important ethical, theological and biblical foundations for my work in the Church, for my work on behalf of justice, and for my work as a moral and constructive theologian.

In 1988, I had the privilege of being invited to participate in a symposium to celebrate the fifteenth anniversary of the publication of *A Theology of Liberation*. A book entitled *The Future of Liberation Theology – Essays in Honor of Gustavo Gutiérrez* (1989), edited by Otto Maduro and Marc Ellis, gathers the presentations made at the symposium. My participation in that symposium gave me the opportunity to re-read in its entirety the second edition of *A Theology of Liberation*, a reading informed by academic theological studies I was completing at the time. It was also a reading guided by my desire to make my own contribution to theology of liberation from the perspective of *mujerista* theology – a theology I had started to elaborate at the beginning of the 1980s grounded in the religious understandings and practices of Latinas living in the USA.

It is important to mention that, since, Gutiérrez has kept writing and I have kept reading his work and I bring to my third reading of *A Theology of Liberation* his further elaborations of earlier themes. In other words, I find it impossible to re-read this book apart from the whole body of work of Gutiérrez. Also, an important factor in this third reading is my keen awareness of the pressure from Church authorities under which Gutiérrez has lived for many, many years. The added explanatory footnotes in the second edition and the reworked section in Chapter 12 are attempts, I believe, to quiet some of the virulent criticisms he has suffered, as well as indicating developments in his own thinking.

In what follows I concentrate on parts of this book that have had particular relevance for my own work as a *mujerista* theologian. First, I point out a few areas in which I am in agreement with Gutiérrez. Then I move to areas where I think differently from him. 'Different' does not mean contradictory nor does it necessarily indicate disagreement. (I could only ascertain whether I disagree with Gutiérrez if I had the opportunity to dialogue with him about our differences.) Second, even in these areas that I articulate differently, I am deeply indebted to the work of Gutiérrez. Certainly his thought continues to play a central role in the moves I make in my arguments, which I ground in my own lived-experience and the experience of my community of struggle and accountability, Latina women living in the USA.

Reading *A Theology of Liberation* today – areas of agreement

In 1988, when I read the second edition of *A Theology of Liberation*, I was impressed by Gutiérrez's faithfulness to the Roman Catholic Church and to its teachings. As an advocate for the ordination of women in the Catholic Church and as one who stresses Latinas' religious understandings and practices instead of concentrating only on official Church teaching in my theological work, I have experienced personally (but only minimally compared to Gutiérrez) the rejection of my work by those in charge in the Church. My own experience of being marginalized by the Church has made me realize and admire Gutiérrez's struggle throughout his life to remain within the Church, to continue to minister as a priest, and to persist in his work as a theologian in the Church. In 1968, at the assembly of the Latin American Bishops Conference in Medellín, Columbia, Gutiérrez was one of the *periti* – one of the expert theologians working with the bishops on the documents issued at the end of that gathering. Ten years later, in 1979, when the Latin American Bishops Conference met again, this time in Puebla, Mexico, Gutiérrez was not invited as a *peritus* but rather participated in a parallel gathering we simply refer to as 'Pueblita' (little Puebla). It was a meeting of those of us who had no direct way of having a say at the bishops' gathering. We worked on voicing issues and elaborating theological under-standings in an attempt to influence the bishops, but we had to do so from the outside, not as an integral part of the process. I remember well the evening gatherings of those of us present at 'Pueblita' and the trips between downtown Puebla where we met and the seminary on the outskirts of the city where the bishops were secluded. Gutiérrez, along with many others of us, worked indefatigably for the Church and as Church. Those of us participating in 'Pueblita' believed that the Church had moved backwards since Medellín and we took seriously our responsibility of calling the Church to be a prophetic voice in the world. We still hoped, back then, that a young John Paul II would not close the windows of the Church John XXIII had thrown open, but that he would recognize and welcome the signs of the times that indicated the need for the Church to push forward in its commitment to the poor, in its commitment to the gospel message of justice.

The second thing that I noticed in my 1988 reading of *A Theology of Liberation* was the breadth and depth of Gutiérrez's scholarship. I had always respected and celebrated his intel-lectual keenness and his willingness to take risks in his advo-cacy for the poor, in his unflinching commitment to justice. The second time around, however – probably because I had grown in appreciation of scholarliness due to my own studies, and because by then I knew well how demanding thorough research is – I grew in admiration of Gutiérrez. Consistently and tirelessly he has presented inspiring and scholarly readings of scripture as well as of the official theological understandings of the Roman Catholic Church. His genius has been to make very clear how both of these call for an effective commitment to justice for the poor, and how the central understandings of liberation theology are truly in line with the best of the Roman Catholic tradition. I realized when I read Gutiérrez's book for the second time how the theology of liberation is an attempt to bring the Church into the modern world as John XXIII had asked. *A Theology of Liberation* is part of the *aggiornamento* Vatican II promoted and embraced. This realization also made me see clearly that it is precisely the fact that Church authorities turned their back on Vatican II that has marginalized liberation theology and the struggles for justice.

As I read once again, in 2007, Gutiérrez's book, I am struck by how well the three meanings or approaches to the process of liberation that he outlines in Chapter 1 have stood the test of time. Those of us who have come to the struggle for liberation from a different form of oppression than poverty – from sexism, ethnic discrimination, racism, heterosexism, ageism, etc. – are able to use the insights he provided more than 35 years ago. We know that our struggles for liberation express our desires as oppressed people, which highlight the conflict that exists between the oppressed and the oppressors. We know that the struggle for liberation places the responsibility to bring about justice on our shoulders, on the shoulders of those of us who are oppressed as well as on those who stand in solidarity with us. We know that it is in and through *la lucha* – the struggle for justice – that human life flourishes. Finally, the struggle for liberation, no matter which form of oppression one is addressing, enriches our understanding of the Bible, our understanding of what it means to say that Jesus saves, of how we are called to contribute to the process of liberation-salvation by expending ourselves to create the conditions necessary for justice to become a concrete reality in everyone's life.

Always aware that any reading is an engaging of my subjective understandings with those of the author, I am particularly conscious of this dynamic as I re-read Part 2 of *A Theology of Liberation*. In my copy this section is heavily underlined for two reasons. First, I continue to try to find an effective praxis, that is to say, effective ways to struggle against oppression and create at least a modicum of justice. Second, from a theological perspective, it is important to see, to highlight, to point out, and to insist on the interconnections between liberation and salvation, which I believe is the main focus of this section of the book. As Gutiérrez says, Christianity has to do away with false dualisms such as temporal–spiritual, profane–sacred, natural–supernatural. I read Part 2 as a call to Christians to live an integrated life, as a call to understand that salvation history is the faith perspective, the lens of our religious beliefs as Christians through which we must see and live everyday life.

This understanding, I suggest, is essential if religious beliefs are to become operative in all spheres of life. I am not talking of a life consumed by or filled with religious practices. Rather I insist on seeing all we do as a religious practice because of the significance we give to what we do, because of the goals we pursue in our daily lives. The arguments Gutiérrez presents here are amplified and made more explicit in another of his books, *The Power of the Poor in History* (1983). In this other book he elaborates the main ideas discussed in Part 2 of *A Theology of Liberation*: theology and ethics are indissolubly united; our relationship with God is not apart from our relationship with the poor; and to sin is to opt for oppression, to create unjust relationships.

These understandings, for me, undergird a central concept of all liberation theologies, that of *proyecto histórico* – historical project. In elaborating an understanding of an historical project for *mujerista* theology, I take into consideration ideas presented by Gutiérrez in Part 2, Chapter 3. First, he makes clear that in all sectors of humankind, particularly among the poor, more and more persons have become and are becoming aware of being active historical subjects. This means that we have come to understand and take responsibility for creating the social conditions needed for liberation – what I call, the flourishing of life. What Gutiérrez emphasizes here is the need to be involved in all spheres of society in order to influence the shape society takes, in order to influence what becomes normative for society. He talks about the importance of being involved in the political sphere, using political in the broad sense, which has to do with who has power and how power is used in society. Gutiérrez insists that we all are human artisans, creators of our reality. Second, he calls for this involvement to be a radical praxis, a way of acting and being that revolves around the axis liberation–oppression, moving to bring about radical structural changes so liberation can become the whole horizon of society. This radical social praxis is indeed the work of Christians: what we need to do and how we need to live in order to embrace Christ's salvation.

The theological basis for these proposals is greatly amplified and developed in Chapter 9 where Gutiérrez insists that the growth of the Kingdom (sic) of God happens when liberation – a historical process – flourishes. He makes painfully clear that the process of liberation, however, will not be able to bring about full justice, for liberation is 'growth of the Kingdom' but it is not all of salvation and, therefore, it is not *the* coming of the Kingdom, which is a gift from God.

Today, Latin American liberation theology is being chided for not having a clear historical project. It is wrongly accused of having made socialism its historical project, and since the fall of the Berlin Wall in 1989 liberation theology is said to have no specific *proyecto histórico*. It seems to me that what Latin American liberation theologians endorsed was not any one so-called socialist regime that existed before the fall of the Berlin Wall or exists today. What they insist on is the need to recognize and radically change the oppressive structures of the capitalist system. The most that can be logically deduced from the theological-ethical understandings of Gutiérrez is that the prevalent economic system of the First World, capitalism, a system that affects all aspects of civil and political society, has to be radically changed if liberation-salvation is to flourish. Gutiérrez is not proposing this or that political and/or economic system but rather is calling for radical change in no matter what system if that system creates and upholds oppression, if it disempowers large sectors of society, if it continues to maintain the oppressive status quo. My purpose in saying this is not to defend Gutiérrez but rather to clarify how I read, understand and use the concepts of history, salvation, historical subject/moral agent, oppression-liberation and radical praxis in my own work.

A third re-reading points out differences

I differ from Gutiérrez in how broadly he conceptualizes radical praxis. In forty years as an activist-theologian what I have come to see is the need to break down this concept of radical praxis into manageable goals. Yes, radical structural change is the goal but we can effectively accomplish only small radical changes that, we hope, can be woven into a whole. This is not easy, I realize, for radical change in one sphere can effectively be reversed unless other concomitant areas have also undergone such change. However, though it is not easy, I do believe that this is the way we must proceed, given the mammoth and all-encompassing power of ideological and economic globalization. Radical praxis today has to be, I would suggest, along the lines of a non-reformist reform, as the French sociologist André Gorz suggested: revolutionary reform geared to radical structural change that does not merely bring about accommodations to the status quo, but which, I believe, takes into consideration the partiality of all human enterprise.

Another understanding in which I differ from Gutiérrez's viewpoint concerns the definition of theology, the purpose of theology, and who are the theologians. Gutiérrez's description of theology is rich and ample. He starts by saying that theology refers to understanding faith and that the function of theology – its purpose and/or goal – is critical reflection on historical praxis geared to the transformation of the world. The reflection, he says, is on 'basic human principles'. Theology for Gutiérrez is a critical theory 'worked out in the light of the Word [of God] accepted in faith and inspired by a practical purpose – and therefore indissolubly linked to historical praxis'. Theology for Gutiérrez is 'reflection, a critical attitude. Theology, follows; it is a second step' (p. 9).

Much of what Gutiérrez says grounds my own understanding; it has been active yeast for my own thinking about theology. Relying on my own experience as an activist theologian, I have adopted and adapted much of what Gutiérrez says about theology. Where I differ from Gutiérrez lies in his statement that theology is a second step, that it is reflection on praxis. Seeing theology as a second step, I would suggest, introduces a discontinuity between action and reflection that is not supported by human experience. Human activity – except routines that are done without thinking like brushing your teeth – requires reflection, and reflection leads to action, for even non-action is a form of action. Here I follow what Antonio Gramsci carefully explains, how I cannot even raise a hand without intellectual work, without my intellect telling the nerves and muscles in my body to move in a given way. This is why Gramsci considers everyone an 'organic intellectual'. (Gramsci also includes the understanding of 'organic intellectual' that Gutiérrez uses to mean those intellectuals who are committed to the historical reality they are immersed in, to the problems and issues of the people among whom they live.)

I understand praxis not as action that needs a second step, reflection (in this case that reflection is what is considered 'theology'). I understand praxis to be reflective action. Reflection both arises from action and leads to more action. Thus it is not a matter of 'first praxis, then reflection'. Praxis is reflective action and, therefore, theology is praxis. Theology has to do with knowledge, and I follow Ignacio Ellacuría in understanding that to acquire – to create – knowledge, one needs to be involved in the material mediations of what is, in this case, Christian faith. Being immersed in one's faith, that is, living it, one apprehends what one believes and the implications of such beliefs; then, in the midst of the immersion and as one apprehends, one begins to elucidate and elaborate one's beliefs. This elucidation and elaboration – putting into words, creating knowledge – changes reality, for what I apprehend does not pass through me as through a funnel. My being immersed, my apprehending and elaborating what I am immersed in, changes reality. Doing theology involves this whole process, not only the third 'moment', not only the elaboration, the putting into words.

Understanding that 'doing theology' is a praxis makes reflection on religious belief the work of historical subjects, of moral agents, that take responsibility for who they are and what they do, which is not apart from what they know and from their religious beliefs. For women, and particularly for marginalized and minoritized women as are Latinas in the USA, to do theology, then, is a self-defining act; to be recognized as 'organic theologians' is part of our struggle to have dominant groups in Church and society recognize our capacity to think, to elucidate and articulate what we believe. Simply put, Latinas can tell you who God is and what God is like just as well as we can clean churches and iron altar linens!

It is true that what I refer to as 'academic theologians', like myself, have access to knowledge generated by many others and have the know-how to elaborate reflection on religious beliefs with broader strokes. I am not saying that academic theologians do not have a specific function. What I want to insist on, however, is that such a function is not necessarily better or always more appropriate, richer or more important than the theology of grassroots people. I agree with Gutiérrez that academic theologians are also called to be 'organic theologians'. But here Gutiérrez is using a second meaning Gramsci gives to the phrase 'organic intellectual'. Organic intellectuals – what I call 'academic organic intellectuals' – are those involved with the issues of a specific historical moment, which means that they have to keep themselves rooted in communities of struggle. Accordingly, for Gutiérrez, 'organic theologians' are those who reflect on historical praxis, a historical praxis in which religious understandings and practices play a vital role. In this I do agree with Gutiérrez. But grassroots Latinas and other grassroots Christians who reflect on their religious beliefs, for whom religious beliefs are central to their worldview, are also 'organic theologians'.

Theology for me, then, is a praxis. Christian theology is reflection on the religious beliefs and practices of Christians by Christians. I do not see this as an individualistic exercise but as an ecclesial exercise, ecclesial here referring to Christian communities. Theology is a praxis that generates critical knowledge, that is, knowledge that in itself changes reality. Because religious faith as an integral element of salvation history is not apart from human history, the praxis of theology is about questions of ultimate meaning for humans, and as such, the praxis of theology is a historical praxis because as humans we are historical beings.

Recognizing all Christians as potential 'organic theologians' brings up another important point for me that finds little echo in Gutiérrez's work. Theology as praxis reaches beyond the official teachings of the Church, into the understandings of the divine and into questions of ultimate meaning that are not necessarily taken into consideration and are not controlled by the official Church. An example helps to clarify what I mean. As I listen carefully to the prayers of Latinas in my church, I notice that they address God very differently from the way God is addressed in prayers of the official rituals of the Church. The prayers said by priests almost always address God as 'Almighty and Eternal God'. Though I have no doubts that Latinas believe God is powerful and has always been and will always be, their way of relating to God brings to light characteristics of the divine that are ignored by the institutional Church. God for us is very personal and we address the divine using endearing terms such as 'Dear God', 'My God'. When I ask Latinas who God is for them and what God is like, their answers open different understandings of the divine from those taught by the official Church. For Latinas God walks with us and is in a mutual relationship with us. This means that, yes, Latinas influence God and Latinas have a right to expect help from God because of their fidelity to God. This way of understanding and relating to the divine explains why the poor and the oppressed continue to believe in God regardless of the harshness of their lives. If the reality of the world of the men who have written and controlled theology influences what is considered 'official Church theology', the reality of Latinas and of other oppressed people is no less capable of yielding understandings that help us humans know who God is and what God is like. Latinas' and grassroots people's theological praxis, then, goes beyond official Church teaching, enriching all theological praxis. If 'academic theologians', particularly those among us who are 'organic theologians', do not recognize grassroots Christians as 'organic theologians' and learn from them, we will continue to impoverish our own theological praxis and the life of the Church at large.

Concluding remarks

There is so much more that I have learned from *A Theology of Liberation* and from the whole body of work of Gustavo Gutiérrez. I have also learned much from Gustavo Gutiérrez the person. I think back with gratitude to when I first met him. Throughout the four decades since then, our paths have crossed occasionally and he has always been kind enough to remember me. We have mutual friends so I know a little about his personal life, and I have learned as much or more from Gutiérrez himself as I have from his theological work. I have learned much from his faithfulness to the Church, to his ministry as a priest, to his work as a theologian. I continue to admire deeply his commitment to the poor, a commitment that has not diminished with the passing of time. I am always struck by his joyfulness despite how harshly and unfairly he has been treated by Church authorities. Fame and recognition have not affected him personally: deep simplicity remains a very strong characteristic of Gutiérrez. His theological work witnesses to his brilliance and intellectual acumen. I continue to learn from Gutiérrez even when I differ with him because his theological work is based on serious research and emerges from his commitment to justice. A wonderful person, a brilliant scholar, a passionate priest, a clear and compassionate thinker – this is what I know about Gustavo Gutiérrez.

One cannot read without learning something about the author. Re-reading *A Theology of Liberation* provides me with the opportunity to 'visit' with Gutiérrez. Recognizing how much he has impacted my own work, how much he has influenced my own thinking is the best compliment I can pay to this book and its author. And I do so joyfully, with admiration, and with deep gratitude.

References

M. H. Ellis and O. Maduro (eds) (1989), *The Future of Liberation Theology: Essays in Honor of Gustavo Gutiérrez*, Maryknoll: Orbis.

P. Freire (1970), *Pedagogy of the Oppressed*, New York: The Seabury Press.

G. Gutiérrez (1973), *A Theology of Liberation: History, Politics and Salvation*, Maryknoll: Orbis.

G. Gutiérrez (1983), *The Power of the Poor in History: Selected Writings*, Maryknoll: Orbis.

II

IN MEMORY OF . . . IN MEMORY OF . . .

Re-reading and Re-membering

Elaine M. Wainwright

These words 'in memory of . . . ' reverberate within the religious consciousness of most who would bear the name 'Christian' and especially among those for whom daily and/or weekly celebration of the Eucharist is at the core of their spirituality: do this in memory . . . *In memoriam* is also a poignant thread which links the living with those who have been or who remain part of their story or stories, their ancestral story and their sacred story. When the title *In Memory of Her* was emblazoned across the cover of a new book in large white letters in 1983, it came, however, as a surprise or even as a shock to many for whom the 'in memory of . . . ' had become a comfort or a commonplace.

What this title did was to place 'her' rather than 'him' as the one being remembered. It evoked an ancient memory but in doing so, it shifted or displaced remembering in its contemporary context. The book was Elisabeth Schüssler Fiorenza's *In Memory of Her: A Feminist Theological Reconstruction of Christian Origins* (1983) and it appeared as second-wave feminism was beginning to affect theological studies. In this same year in which *In Memory of Her* was first published, I began my postgraduate studies as a New Testament scholar and as a woman whose feminist consciousness was in its nascency. One of the texts which we were required to read in a biblical hermeneutics course was Schüssler Fiorenza's *In Memory of Her*. The impact of this text has been life-shaping for me as a Christian feminist and career-shaping for me as a feminist biblical scholar. As I re-read, I shall also be remembering how my life and scholarship have intersected with the life and scholarship of Elisabeth Schüssler Fiorenza who is both friend and colleague in feminist theological reconstructions of Christian origins.

Evoking re[-]membering/s

The invitation to re-read for this volume has been accompanied by an experience of remembering: remembering the context and experience of my initial reading, remembering the way the text chosen for re-reading has affected not only my scholarship but that of others in my field of expertise. I will, therefore, at the outset of my re-reading explore the *remembering* that my re-reading has evoked. I am aware, however, that there has been a very particular *re-membering* that has characterized scholars' engagement with feminist reconstructions of Christian origins over the past 26 years in which *In Memory of Her* has functioned as a foundational text and I also want to take this into account.

To dedicate or entitle a text *In Memory of* . . . is to remember, to bring back into consciousness one who may have been forgotten or absent from our awareness for some time. *In Memory of Her* brought back to mind the woman who 'anoints' Jesus and the many other women whose stories accompany hers in the Gospels, other New Testament texts, and early Christian literature. To re-member, on the other hand, evokes the re-member-ing, the re-assembling of what has been dis-membered. Such a dis-membering of women is narrated in the violent story of Judges 19 in which an unnamed woman of Bethlehem who is married to a Levite of Gibeah is dismembered by the Levite and sent throughout the tribes of Israel after she has been brutally raped all night by the Benjaminites of the town in which the travellers sought overnight refuge. She represents symbolically the women of the biblical story and of the religious traditions to which that story gave birth who have been dis-membered within their religious communities by way of a silencing of their voices, an excluding of them from their history and narrative, a prescribing of their roles, a rendering of them as invisible, and an enacting of bodily violence against them in many different ways. My act of re-membering seeks to bring together the members, the women members of the *ekklesia*, who have been dis-membered. It recognizes and takes account of the dis-membering, however painful that might be, without becoming submerged in it. On the other hand, however, it also re-members those who have been dis-membered in the androcentric biblical text and in the history of women's engagement in the biblical religions of Judaism and emerging Christianity. To do this is to be a feminist critic walking the path of deconstruction with the tools of a hermeneutic of suspicion in one hand, and the path of reconstruction with the tools of a hermeneutic of remembrance in the other. And it is the two faces of remembering and re-membering which *In Memory of Her* holds up to me as I re-read.

Undertaking the task of re-reading evokes myriads of memories that indicate how personal and professional life-paths intertwine. I had consciously embarked on a feminist journey just three or four years prior to my taking up postgraduate studies at the Catholic Theological Union in Chicago in 1983 where I initially encountered *In Memory of Her*. As I was searching for a focus for an honours thesis addressing hermeneutics and justice, my supervisor handed me a copy of Phyllis Trible's *God and the Rhetoric of Sexuality* (1986). The reading of Trible's text opened my eyes to the intersection of justice and feminism at a most profound level which has been life-changing and which has directed my scholarship since that time. In that honours thesis, I was searching for hermeneutical principles that would enable me to adjudicate conflicting claims for biblical teachings on contemporary justice issues both in the academy in which I was working and in the political context in which I was living. Turning that search toward emerging feminism sent me on a journey which readied me for encounter with *In Memory of Her*.

Excitement and expectation characterized my move to Chicago in that latter half of 1983. At the Catholic Theological

Union, I encountered women who were on a similar journey to the one I had begun in recognizing feminism as a constitutent element of justice. Stimulating conversations ranged over issues such as women's ordination, language of liturgy, violence against women, and the social and ecclesial structures that masked such violence. And in October of that year, 'From Generation to Generation: Woman-Church Speaks', the first Women-Church conference, took place in the city with hundreds of women gathering, celebrating liturgically, engaging theologically and generating an extraordinary spirit of hope for a new future for women of the *ekklesia* and for women of the Catholic tradition within that broader *ekklesia*. I saw in person and heard the voices of women who had only been names on scholarly articles and books – Rosemary Radford Ruether, Elisabeth Schüssler Fiorenza, Joan Chittister and Teresa Kane, to name but a few. There was a spirit abroad that gave hope and a new vision for women both socially and ecclesially and a recognition that we could participate in the shaping of that vision and that future. It was in such a context of a significant expansion of my personal consciousness as a woman in the Church that I read *In Memory of Her* for the first time.

The significance of that first reading is revealed to me now when I return to my 1983 copy. It is highlighted on almost every page, underlined and with pencil comments and questions in the margins. The insights and the questions seem almost to tumble over one another in a way that reminds me of that initial experience. The book itself reveals this as books are among my most valued possessions. I treasure them and the treasures which they open up to us and so rarely do I mark them in any way. And yet *In Memory of Her* is completely marked. Here was a work that was dealing in depth with the questions with which my small honours thesis was beginning to engage just a few years earlier. Here was a work which could become a map for the journey I was embarking on as a feminist biblical scholar.

As this chapter unfolds, I will engage more concretely with the content of this foundational text for feminist biblical hermeneutics. Here, however, I wish simply to point to two aspects of the journey of this text to which reference will also be made as we proceed. On the one hand, *In Memory of Her* has been like a beacon whose light has guided many scholars who have undertaken the myriad of feminist interpretations of biblical texts and reconstructions of Christian origins that have emerged over more than two decades. A key moment in this unfolding of Elisabeth Schüssler Fiorenza's work was the presentation to her of three *festschrifts* in her honour at the Society of Biblical Literature meeting in 2003: *Toward A New Heaven and a New Earth* (2003), *Walk in the Ways of Wisdom* (2003), and *On the Cutting Edge* (2004). On the other hand, Schüssler Fiorenza's work has been like a lightening rod, attracting criticisms that are not just those which characterize our discipline and enhance our work but which have caricatured her approaches and her contribution to scholarship. As scholar of excellence and woman of integrity, she has negotiated her way through all such waters so that she too is now re[-]membered.

Enacting and embracing re[-]membering – theological and hermeneutical journeys

Forgetting in all its manifestations can be an act of dismembering which functions very subtly. Elisabeth Schüssler Fiorenza brings such *forgetting* before her readers as *In Memory of Her* opens and she re-members the woman who poured ointment over the head of Jesus who has been forgotten in the history and theologizing of the Church while the betrayer of Jesus, Judas, has been remembered. Re-reading the book's opening paragraph brought back to my mind an experience I had some years after my initial reading which confirmed Schüssler Fiorenza's claim. I was invited to speak to the Australian Catholic Bishops Conference in April 1988. I used the example of the woman of Mark 14.3–9 to demonstrate how women and women's stories can be overlooked in reading the biblical story and can be excluded from lectionaries. I contrasted her with Judas who betrayed and Peter who denied Jesus. In question time, the Chairperson of the Conference asked if I was implying that this woman was overlooked or excluded because she was a woman. He proceeded to point out that this was not so. We remembered Judas and Peter, he explained, not because they were male disciples but because they had betrayed and denied. It seems that in this instance faithful discipleship as manifest in a woman must give precedence to the betrayal and denial of key male characters regardless of the fact that the Gospel text does not say, 'Truly I say to you, wherever the gospel is told in the whole world, what Judas and Peter have done will be told in memory of them.' A clear example of the conscious or unconscious dis-membering of women, textually and theologically!

Since 1983, there has been much remembering and re-membering as feminist biblical scholars of early Christian origins have re-read and reconstructed the discipleship of women of the *basileia* movement around Jesus and the engagement of women in mission as this movement spread beyond Palestine into Syria, Asia Minor and to Rome. Initially, studies focused on particular stories, particular female characters of the New Testament texts, and many articles began to appear as feminist scholars engaged the hermeneutical and methodological issues raised by *In Memory of Her*. The story of the woman of Mark 14.3–9 which gave Schüssler Fiorenza her title, but which is not extensively explored in her text, is but one example of the many texts which have attracted significant scholarly attention and investigation since 1983. In my own recent scholarship, I have returned to a study of Mark 14.3–9 and its possible parallels in the other Gospels (Matt. 26.6–13; Luke 7.36–50; and John 12.1–8), and this has provided me with the opportunity to survey the feminist analyses of these texts over the last two decades. Not surprisingly, it is characterized by the range of methodological approaches that are typical of feminist biblical interpretation. In my own re-readings of the four different stories of this woman with *myron*, the use of intertextuality as an interpretive tool enabled me to read the action of the woman as narrated in the Gospels of Mark and Matthew as a gesture of healing. A nuancing of my feminist hermeneutic with ecological, postcolonial and Queer perspectives and questions demonstrates the complex developments that have emerged in feminist biblical interpretations of early Christian texts and reconstructions of the history of women of that emerging Christian world. In all of this, the work begun by Elisabeth Schüssler Fiorenza has borne fruit far beyond her imaginings. There has been a re[-]membering of not one but of many if not all the stories of women from early Christianity, resulting in a wealth of articles and books which it is hoped will counter the forgetting that gave rise to the second wave of feminist biblical interpretation which Schüssler Fiorenza's *In Memory of Her* symbolizes.

In keeping with Schüssler Fiorenza's own vision for her book, *In Memory of Her* provided me and many other scholars with 'building blocks and road maps'. Her approach was significantly historical and it carried the twofold goal of restoring women's stories to the history of emerging Christianity and of reclaiming this restored history for women as well as men. The work of restoration was, therefore, to be both academic, in that it would participate in the work of New Testament scholars and historians of early Christianity, and effective beyond academia, in that it would empower women of the *ekklesia* with a restored history or genealogy in which they and their foresisters had a place. Re-reading this twofold goal that has accompanied my own scholarship across the decades, I was reminded of the day that I suddenly came to the recognition that my imagined or constructed world of early Christianity had been populated by men, shaped as it had been by decades of theological, ecclesial and academic constructions or re-constructions. It was a stark realization that gave further impetus for the scholarly and personal path I was beginning to follow.

I wanted to restore women to early Christian history through the study of a particular Gospel and so, with *In Memory of Her* in hand, I embarked upon a feminist re-reading of the Gospel of Matthew. In the mid-1980s, the new narrative criticism provided tools beyond those envisaged in the more historical emphases of *In Memory of Her*. These tools enabled me to study the female characters of the Gospel of Matthew so that those characters could be restored to the Gospel and that their stories could be seen to form a sub-text which critiqued the dominant androcentric and patriarchal emphases of the Gospel as a whole. Combining this with a redaction-critical study enabled me to reconstruct the traditioning of the stories of women through dialogue with data emerging about women's roles and functions within the Graeco-Roman society of the first century. From this layered study, it was possible to make tentative claims about women's participation in the shaping of the Matthean Gospel. Such a study, grounded as it was in the feminist hermeneutic of Elisabeth Schüssler Fiorenza but including a new configuration of methodological approaches, was able not only to restore women to early Christian history but also to restore the stories of women to the Gospel text.

This work was published in the early 1990s and took its place among a number of similar volumes given to the study of the female characters of Gospels and other early Christian texts. Among some of the feminist scholars whose work characterized this decade marked by varied approaches to women in the Gospels, to name just one category, are Hisako Kinakawa, Monika Fander, Turid Karlsen Seim, Barbara Reid, Dorothy Lee, Emily Cheney, Colleen Conway, Adeleine Fehribach and many others. Further examples of such scholarship across not only the New Testament but other early Christian texts can be found in the second volume of *Searching the Scriptures*, edited by Elisabeth Schüssler Fiorenza in 1994, and demonstrative, as I have been saying, of the scholarship that *In Memory of Her* has generated. Hermeneutical and methodological sophistication and nuance was emerging within the field of feminist interpretations and reconstructions of early Christianity and finding expression in feminist critical monographs that could take their place alongside and be brought into dialogue with the many different approaches to particular books of the New Testament and texts of early Christianity. The door which *In Memory of Her* opened was becoming much more difficult to close.

The goal, however, of Elisabeth Schüssler Fiorenza and a growing number of feminist scholars of the New Testament and early Christianity was not only re[-]membering women of antiquity into the present but also decentring biblical scholarship. It was not enough for our books to be taking their places on the shelves of scholarly libraries. It was important that our work shift the centre of the discipline, that it be ethical. In this, as in her contribution to the initial development of feminist biblical hermeneutics, Schüssler Fiorenza was a leader. In *But She Said: Feminist Practices of Biblical Interpretation*, published in 1992, she began to chart a shift that was happening elsewhere in feminist studies. Women of colour and of different ethnic, socio-economic and religious groups were entering the field of feminist studies. They were drawing attention to the problematic of the term 'woman' as a universal as it failed to take account of the differences among women, of the intersecting and interstructural layers of domination that characterize the lives of women and men. In 1992, Schüssler Fiorenza introduced the term *kyriarchy* into feminist biblical interpretation, demonstrating by way of an analysis of patriarchal Greek democracy, how the interstructural layering of domination provides a lens for reading early Christianity as well as the contemporary *ekklesia*. Seeds sown in *In Memory of Her* were beginning to grow into young shoots and to put out runners in different direction thus realizing the potential in the seeds which we encountered in 1983.

Her developing work was demonstrating that feminist biblical interpretation was not simply an academic movement providing theoretical tools for gendered analyses of texts and contexts but that it was a political movement as well, seeking emancipation not only of women but of all who were trapped in the manifold layers of oppressive kyriarchy. Such emancipation which placed biblical scholarship in a position of responsibility to the public square also extended back into analyses of texts which must include a study of the complex intersections of oppression in New Testament texts and constructions of early Christianity. The work of Schüssler Fiorenza sought to hold together the arena of the public aspect of biblical scholarship with the public dimensions of women's personal and ecclesial lives demonstrating the feminist maxim that the personal is truly political. I became aware once again of how significant these developments have been very recently when I co-taught a course called The Gendered Church. I found myself continually drawing attention to the fact that analyses of gender alone will not lead to change. Rather, insights from feminist studies generally and from feminist biblical and theological studies in particular demonstrate that the deconstructive/reconstructive processes which characterize those studies must also inform the praxis which accompanies and is the outcome of such theologizing. Such critical analyses of gender must also include critical engagement with the other markers of the lives of women and men, culture and ethnicity being two such additional categories that characterize each class I teach in my current context of Aotearoa New Zealand, a bi-cultural nation on the edge of Oceania. Only in this way will both society and scholarship be changed.

This is to remind me of how my own personal and scholarly journey has continued to intersect since the early 1980s when I began my encounter with feminist biblical scholarship and my personal journey of transformation. My engagement with the burgeoning scholarship in feminist biblical studies and theology was shifting my own consciousness. I have already made reference to the sudden awareness in these early stages of my journey that my constructed world of early Christianity had been peopled by men and that this was beginning to shift as I encountered the women of the biblical text and tradition. I also associate with Chicago, my first spontaneous spiritual encounter with God imaged female – an experience that came upon me in a way which surprised me at the same time that it reminded me of the Sophia-God of Jesus whom readers of *In Memory of Her* encounter as the female gestalt of God. Such personal transformations impelled me as a teacher to want to share knowledge as well as provide experiences for women and men who have been and who are seeking liberation from the oppressive manifestations of kyriarchy. This has entailed the development and teaching of courses as well as the providing of workshops that enable participants to engage with the wealth of scholarship that has increasingly adorned my bookshelves since *God and the Rhetoric of Sexuality* and *In Memory of Her* had almost sole right to space. Such contexts also provide the potential for transformations of consciousness to take place as my own experience attested. Also since the rhetorical effect of the androcentric language and imagery of the biblical and theological tradition had been demonstrated and critiqued not only by Schüssler Fiorenza but by many others as well as being experienced by ecclesial women, I have been engaged with a small group of women in translating the scriptures for Sunday liturgies in the Catholic Church calendar into inclusive language. Together we, the members of this small group, recognize the limited scope of this task but if it is taken up in parishes as constitutive of their commitment to transformation of all that is unjust among them, then it can contribute to their ethical journey of transformation and lead to making all the language of liturgy inclusive.

To undertake such journeys inviting transformation in scholarship, among our peers in academia as well as among those who share our ecclesial settings, is not without its costs. I vividly remember seeing Elisabeth Schüssler Fiorenza scorned by a colleague after a paper she gave at the 1986 SNTS meeting in Atlanta. Her questioner began his remarks with a sarcastic 'I would have expected you to have arrived where you did . . .' I remember being shocked and only later realized that anyone who heard Raymond Brown's paper that same morning on whether any of the many first- or second-century Gospels apart from Matthew, Mark, Luke and John were canonical could well have begun a question with the same remark but, of course, no one did that. It seemed that it was acceptable to scorn the work of emerging feminist biblical scholars. Traditional scholarship and its personnel demanded much more respect. This experience heralded for me the long road which I too have travelled beyond that 1986 meeting during which my academic and ecclesial work and their intersections have lead to scorn, ridicule and many other tactics which emerge in response to the challenging of paradigms that are often held as truth-claims. It is the cost of working for transformation and it is borne most heavily not by myself or others like me but by those whose worlds are in most need of transformation. Such costs were not as evident in the hope-filled days of 1983. They have, however, forged bonds which have sustained women scholars and activists in the long journey that re[-]membering entails. One nuanced recollection these reflections evoke is the enjoyment that Elisabeth experienced as visiting lecturer to Brisbane in the late 1990s when her lecture was picketed by those who had placed leaflets on car windscreens at various Eucharists in Catholic parishes the previous day warning of the evils of her scholarship. It was her first picket! Needless to say, the same enjoyment was not shared by me as her host as I spent the day of the lecture negotiating my way through the various ecclesial authorities to ensure that the lecture went ahead and in the designated venue. In retrospect, of course, the memory brings a smile but is also reminiscent of the resistance that has characterized the re[-]membering of her.

On her pathway of transforming biblical scholarship beyond 1983, Schüssler Fiorenza has engaged with a range of feminist, feminist biblical and feminist theological scholars. Feminist biblical scholars, for instance, were beginning to employ the new literary critical methods as I indicated above. Schüssler Fiorenza was cautious of such approaches if they were not infused with a critical feminist recognition of the kyriocentric nature of the text and the accompanying nuancing of the approach that was needed so that women did not become entrapped in or limited by the horizons of the text. The shift or the turn which she was beginning to make in her own paradigm was toward rhetoric or the rhetorical. My re-reading of *In Memory of Her* brought me to an awareness of its rudimentary character in the development of Schüssler Fiorenza's approach over the decades and how much its insights have been developed and more finely nuanced. The hermeneutical framework which she proposed in *In Memory of Her* was that of the foundational feminist paradigm: a hermeneutics of suspicion and a hermeneutics of remembrance or reclamation. I am reminded that it was only a year later, in 1984 in *Bread not Stone*, that she extended her feminist hermeneutic to include those of proclamation and of creative imagination. These latter two aspects of the framework demonstrate her recognition that the work of feminist biblical scholars is theological and entails the restoration of women within the context of the *ekklesia*: its proclamation and its creative representation of women informed by the work of feminist biblical scholars and theologians. This fourfold hermeneutical paradigm has, I have realized, informed my own scholarship, my teaching and my engagement in the *ekklesia* since the mid-1980s. It informs not only what I do but who I am.

The turn to rhetoric evident in Schüssler Fiorenza's more

recent work seems a significant shift from the hermeneutic frame of *In Memory of Her* and yet on closer analysis it is more a nuancing of it. Her *Rhetorics of Liberation* closely resembles a *Hermeneutics of Suspicion* in that it seeks to uncover the oppressive structures and relationships of power in text, context and history of interpretation, a task which I remember finding almost overwhelming in its extent on my first reading of *In Memory of Her* in 1983. Some of that task being accomplished, I am confronted now not so much with its extent but its ongoing imperative – this is a task we must never forget as text, context and history of interpretation will retain their kyriocentricity and hence we will need to ensure that our reading is always against their grain. A *Rhetorics of Differences* parallels the *Hermeneutics of Remembrance* but it goes beyond the reclamation of women and their story to include the remembering of women and men of different colour, race, class and religion. Shifting to a *Rhetorics of Equality* provides a lens informed by the 'democratic' vision of the *basileia* to examine how the biblical text is used or how it functions in the *ekklesia*. This is but a nuanced articulation of the *Hermeneutics of Proclamation*. The type of future envisioned for the *ekklesia* and the creative ways of articulating these visions are simply nuanced or emphasized differently in each of the *Rhetorics of Vision* and the *Hermeneutics of Creative Imagination*. In *Wisdom's Ways*, published in 2001, almost twenty years after *In Memory of Her*, the hermeneutical and rhetorical aspects of Schüssler Fiorenza's work coalesce as she invites others to become engaged with her in Wisdom's dance of interpretation, a public/political act which must be characterized by an ethic of inclusion and life-enhancement for all. The *basileia* vision understood in a contemporary context of liberation is what must inform the interpretive task.

Re-reading *In Memory of Her* reminded me again of how profoundly the engagement with Elisabeth Schüssler Fiorenza's scholarship has formed and transformed my own scholarship and it evoked memories of hermeneutical and theological journeys. Her feminist hermeneutical model of suspicion and remembrance and her biblical paradigm of prototype which I encountered first in *In Memory of Her* and *Bread not*

Stone were foundational to my feminist study of the women of Matthew's Gospel, *Towards a Feminist Critical Reading of the Gospel according to Matthew*. Attention to difference which her model of kyriarchy made manifest became the key characteristic of the reading paradigm I developed to facilitate a feminist rereading of the Matthean Jesus in *Shall We Look for Another?* (1998). I wanted to listen for different understandings of Jesus that would emerge from different reading positions. This goal turned my attention to the differences in the house churches or smaller reading communities that constituted the Matthean community at large: the scribal, the more egalitarian and the poorer communities. Seeking to read from their different locations enabled me to hear metaphors and characterizations of Jesus that doctrinal and historical critical theological readings have obscured. The recognition that gender must always be examined in conjunction with race, class and religion that characterized Schüssler Fiorenza's developing hermeneutical paradigm informed my construction of a reading framework to examine the genderization of healing in early Christianity. This work emerged as *Women Healing/Healing Women* in 2006. In it, a gender-critical perspective was combined with aspects of postcolonial and ecological studies to facilitate a study of women's engagement in healing in early Christianity. My emerging text is, however, rhetorical as well as historical in its concern as to how the ancient healing women and the products of the Earth with which they interact are reconstructed and how our re-reading of them might shape a new consciousness that is inclusive of not only the human but the other-than-human as well.

One aspect of Elisabeth Schüssler Fiorenza's hermeneutical and theological journey that has developed beyond *In Memory of Her* is that of the public nature of contemporary biblical studies. Her fourfold rhetorical framework makes it clear that biblical and theological studies do not belong just in the academic critical reconstruction of early Christianity and the restoration of women's stories to that construction. Rather, she has made clear that biblical interpretation is continually taking place in the *ekklesia* in a way that impacts the square or the marketplace. Her understanding of the *ekklesia*, based as it is on the patriarchal Greek democratic model, provides a framework that can enable biblical scholars and theologians to engage in public theology. This is an area which I am just beginning to explore together with colleagues in national and international networks. A paper I gave very recently in a context which engaged parliamentarians and theologians demonstrated the value of the *ekklesia* as a tool for the study of gender and democracy. As this aspect of my own work develops, my dialogue with Schüssler Fiorenza's more recent work in which she explores the *public* and *ethical* aspects of feminist theological scholarship will likewise become more nuanced.

Beyond re[-]membering

As this re[-]membering of hermeneutical and theological journeys has unfolded I have recalled the initial reading of *In Memory of Her* and sought to replay the experience of re-reading 26 years on. Memories have intersected with shifts and changes in the theological landscape and the personal and the political refuse to be separated. On arriving at this point where I look beyond re[-]membering, I am conscious of all that has not been said. I have not addressed the centrality of the *basileia* vision of Jesus in my own biblical scholarship, in my proclamation of the text in the context of preaching, and in my spirituality as a Christian feminist – that vision which Schüssler Fiorenza brought to the fore in *In Memory of Her*. Another thread that has woven through the layers of my life and scholarship has been that of Sophia, the female gestalt of God in the Wisdom literature and one manifestation of the God of Jesus in the Gospel traditions. She has been guide, companion and friend as well as beacon to continually remind me and to remind us of the dis-membering of images of God in the biblical text and tradition and the task of re-membering that must take place.

This final memory sends me back to 1983 and the appearance of *In Memory of Her*. Since that time, much has been achieved. The women of the New Testament and early Christianity have been re-membered. They have been returned to the texts in which their stories are told and that text has been reconstructed and reclaimed rhetorically in order to return women to early Christianity so that it is the history of women and men. Radical engagement with feminist critical paradigms for biblical interpretation by women of colour and women from a wide range of context across the globe has lead to the development of not one but many differently nuanced approaches. From these and other dialogue between and among Elisabeth Schüssler Fiorenza and other feminist scholars across disciplines, feminist critical paradigms of interpretive reading and reconstruction have been developed that have been employed in variously nuanced ways across ranges of projects that could never have been envisaged in 1983. Such readings and reconstructions are not only taking place in the academy but in ecclesial communities around the world. This will continue into the future.

The invitation to re-read and to re[-]member has also made me conscious of the ongoing nature of the task of feminist critical biblical interpretation and theology – it is women's (and men's) work which is never done. We have a public and political task to ensure that the extraordinary work already accomplished through feminist biblical interpretation takes effect in the *ekklesia* and in the *polis*. The personal is indeed political and the work can never cease until not only all women but all women and men are free.

References

E. S. Fiorenza (1983), *In Memory of Her: A Feminist Theological Reconstruction of Christian Origins*, New York: Crossroad.

E. S. Fiorenza (1992), *But She Said: Feminist Practices of Biblical Interpretation*, Boston: Beacon.

E. S. Fiorenza (ed.) (1994), *Searching the Scriptures*, Vol. 2 *A Feminist Commentary*, New York: Crossroad.

E. S. Fiorenza and F. Segovia (eds) (2003), *Toward a New Heaven and a New Earth: Essays in Honor of Elisabeth Schüssler Fiorenza*, Maryknoll: Orbis.

E. S. Fiorenza, S. Matthews, M. Johnson-Debaufre and C. B. Kittredge (eds) (2003), *Walk in the Ways of Wisdom: Essays in Honour of Elisabeth Schüssler Fiorenza*, Harrisburg: Trinity Press International.

J. Schaberg, A. Bach and E. Fuchs (2004), *On the Cutting Edge: The*

Study of Women in Biblical Worlds: Essays in Honor of Elisabeth Schüssler Fiorenza, New York: Continuum.

P. Trible (1986), *God and the Rhetoric of Sexuality*, Minneapolis: Fortress Press.

E. Wainwright (1998), *Shall We Look for Another: A Feminist Reading of the Matthean Jesus*, Maryknoll: Orbis.

E. Wainwright (2006), *Women Healing/Healing Women: The Genderization of Healing in Early Christianity*, New York: Equinox.

12

THE EAGLE AND THE
FEMINIST THEOLOGIAN

Journeying with John

Lisa Isherwood

Who knows which comes first, the chicken or the egg? I feel this
way with my choice of book to re-read – it does seem rather
churlish for a theologian, and particularly one who is not a biblical scholar, to pick a Gospel! But the truth is that it is a book
that has captivated me for many years now and who knows
which came first, the reading of the book or the theologian?

I was first introduced to John's Gospel as an academic study
when I studied for 'A level' at a Catholic school. I was captivated from the outset by what I was told: here was a mystical
book, one that spoke of sacraments and other worlds that could
be brought to bear on our own through magical rituals. A book
that talked of a divided world, divided between good and evil,
those in the light and those not – we took a sophisticated view
of this, my 17-year-old colleagues and I, we knew that there
were those who just knew, who had insight, and others who
just dwelt in sheer ignorance! Whether the spiritually ignorant
deserved hell or not was an endless question that we debated
with the nun who taught us – she had a rather interesting view:
there was a hell, no one was in it and even if they were they
didn't know they were – there is a kindly God, girls!

We were introduced to the 'I am' sayings in the light of the
Prologue which proved to us beyond all doubt that right there
at the beginning of time Jesus, the Word, was united with God

in creation and the utterances about him were revelations about an eternal nature, one fixed in all time, Alpha and Omega. We believed this was illustrated beyond any question in John 14.20 where Jesus told us (no real engagement with author input here!) he was in the Father – we paid less attention to 'and you in me, and I in you', which seemed an affectionate afterthought. We could take comfort in this all-powerful hero who was on our side, if we were on his, because he could face even death for us and emerge triumphant. We realized that we had to be ever mindful of the darkness and could understand that many actions were carried out 'at night' because they were too shameful to be in the light. We may have assumed we grasped this intellectually but there was nevertheless a great deal of moral ambiguity floating around. However, we, girls, all set out to be 'sons of light' and did not bat an eyelid!

I met John again in my undergraduate studies within a liberal Protestant faculty, a setting in which I even approached Raymond Brown, a Catholic scholar of John, with extreme caution. As to the input, I enjoyed it, and I loved having the world of John, for whom I had great affection, expanded. I think the thing that made the most impression was the Zoroastrian influence on the writing which, of course, only confirmed my dualistic world-view in which good and evil battled it out daily, leading to an ultimate show-down. In truth I am not sure that I ever moved much beyond the view given me at school – certainly this was true in the area of John as a Gospel about sacraments. However many tutors and peers questioned my assumption that John, 'above all other Gospels', set before us an elaborate sacramental system, I would not move – my limited Catholic views were in place. No doubt in me either that, within this mystical and magical Gospel, what was being referred to was transubstantiation (John 6.52–58) – why was that so hard to believe, I often wondered. After all, this was a very top-down world and whatever God decided to do he surely could. In addition, of course, given the need of the world to transform itself to come in line with another reality through the leading of the Counsellor, it seemed to be quite acceptable to suggest that sacraments may be a good way to rehearse this alternate reality. In addition to this high view of the sacraments

I also held a rather high view of priesthood even though it was obvious that most did not deserve the praise. I was, I suspect, beginning to wonder why they had to be men.

When I decided to pursue further study in the area of mysticism, it was once again John that provided a starting point. I had by this time taken notice of the phrase 'and you in me and I in you' and begun to wonder if it had anything to offer a study of the mystical way. The intriguing world of those few verses in chapter 17, so far from subsequent Trinitarian doctrine, said more to me about human nature than about the triune and sealed-off, self-sufficient God. What was the purpose of mysticism? How would it at all change the reality we live in? – these were some of the questions in my head at the time. Were mystics the people who were able to live in the world and not of it that John spoke about? Would that shed light on the tension inherent in 'the time is coming and now is' – how could this be possible? I could see that C. H. Dodd wished to call this tension 'realized eschatology' and understood that this phrase had many interpretations, but I was always interested in what the practical outcome may be – what difference did it all make to the world here and now? By this time I had also studied some psychology and was becoming familiar with the idea that 'living as if' could be a very powerful tool in the psychological knapsack but also saw that too much of it led to something very unreal – a world of fairy dust. Surely mystics were not just sprinkling fairy dust? Or is that where the mystical magical gospel had to lead, to a world of higher contemplation that in essence was only that, with no earthly consequences at all? John was not the focus of my study in mysticism but the Gospel was a place that held some questions for me with which to examine the phenomena.

It is undoubtedly true that at the beginning of my study of mysticism I still held a dualistic and hierarchical frame to be the way things were, even if a few cracks were showing at the edges of my thinking. My undergraduate teaching however had placed in me the 'knowledge' that where it did not seem to fit there was probably something wrong with my logic. This hierarchical approach made me believe that some were able to be mystics and they offered their insights to the Church for the edification of the faithful. Perhaps I am being a little harsh on myself there, but roughly speaking this was a starting point. What emerged was an increasing understanding that, far from being the exception, living in the mystical way was for all. I came to see it as the logical outcome of a baptized life. This union with God and in a sense seeing with God's eyes, living what is to come and what seemed to be a Christian life well lived. My research revolved around the monastic rule of St Bernard and how he encouraged his brothers to live lives of union with God, very sensual lives of union as I was surprised to see. So the tension for me was how people living everyday lives could achieve this union – understanding the Song of Songs through metaphysical glasses as the relationship of the soul to God did not at this point give me any clues as to where we may begin. And then for me a revelation – feminist theology. This changed everything for ever as it does for so many people.

The dualistic blinkers came off – it was some time until I decided metaphysics had to go too – and a new world was revealed. In this new light the eschatological tension spoke a language of psychology and theology that would in time for me be one of radical incarnational theology and somatic psychology. God left the heavens once and for all – not a position that other feminists would be happy with, I am well aware. My reading companions in those days were Ruether, Heyward, Brock, Moltmann-Wendel and many others. It was of course Schüssler Fiorenza who helped me with another Johannine puzzle, that of 'the Word'. What had been the very foundations of my Catholic education now became a kidnapping and takeover bid of the worst kind. Behind that innocent and potentially reassuring statement lay a world of power and betrayal, one in which a much older tradition was obliterated. Schüssler Fiorenza, Asphodel Long and many others changed my reading of this book and from it my view of the world. They showed how the Sophia tradition was lost almost in a word, THE WORD, and how this in turn altered everything from God to the way we view each other. In this not so subtle gender change came a God who was now removed rather than Sophia who rolled up her sleeves in the marketplace to live with and between the people. Any notion of a female aspect of the divine was lost in this disembodied Word, this divine dictation, and with it much empowerment of contemporary women. The universal gospel was being unmasked for what it was, a not so universal patriarchal world-view. It was one that did not allow us to enter fully into our prehistory in a way that could help us contextualize our present reality. The female divine that was hidden from view was one that made the world a more mutual place and made the story of 'redemption' a very different one, if it needed to be told at all. After all, the Sophia tradition speaks of unfolding and becoming, not of dramatic falls from grace that take heroic blood sacrifice to put right. This does not just have implications for divine economies but for all kinds of relational economies in the world in which we live and have constructed on the back of our limited and blood-sacrificial understandings. There is also a sensuousness in this book which is unlocked once we do away with the disembodied Word and instead see the main character as Sophia incarnate, one among many brothers and sisters so embodied. The anointing of Jesus by Mary, who has been seen by some as a priestess anointing for burial, and the washing of the disciples' feet by Jesus, become intimate sensuous acts and not hierarchical performances. They show a connection between friends that is deep, trusting and life-giving. It also seems to me that many of the 'I am' sayings take on a different meaning when they are freed to be intimate and sensuous sayings, when they signal intentions of interrelationality and not some already worked-out divine imposition.

My feminist sisters offered many possibilities for this book from female authorship to divine marriage between Jesus (the god) and Mary Magdalene (the goddess). There were also ways to read that allowed a hitherto barely seen very human God/man to emerge, the one who wept real tears and whose passion altered reality. Of course what was also happening was that as I read I realized that there were women in this story and that their part was not insignificant – they were not the mere extras, the literary eye-candy, of my youthful reading, or indeed the annoying ones who just did not get it, the ones that had to have things explained very slowly to them. They were powerful figures who challenged much that was happening and may even be seen to make much of it occur. We have had readings that suggest Mary and Martha were a lesbian couple and indeed a significant couple in the history of early Christianity, yet other readings that suggest that Mary was married to Jesus. All of these readings make my reading of this book a much richer experience and one that can deal with the texts as mythic rather than holy scripture. By this of course I mean mythic in that they are precisely there to grow with the reader and in turn to help the reader grow. They are not the blueprint for understanding an already worked-out faith which is how I was first introduced to them.

For many of my academic contemporaries the Samaritan woman symbolizes the many oppressed and marginalized ethnic groups in our world. The power with which they claim she became empowered in her exchange with Jesus in the story is the power they advocate for all the women who are ethnically oppressed. With this kind of reading I always feel that Jesus is not always the good guy. He often appears to be the unwitting mouthpiece of the oppressive system or a man being led to greater understanding through the lived experience of those around him, including women. The Samaritan woman has been transformed for me from a 'sexual sinner' – this is how we were encouraged to view her – who was forgiven and set free to a woman who owns her own body and with it her own integrity, a woman who would be a good advocate for sexual and ethnic rights. She is one who has lived it and whose life calls for justice and who can work for social change as a result of her experience. The nuns would cringe!

Right at the beginning of this book is the story of Jesus and his mother at a wedding feast. I was taught that this was the divine bridegroom who wed the Church, or indeed the one who would in time become that wine of abundant life offered on the altars of that same Church. The role of his mother in the story was to get it wrong, to be told off and in this way to be the stooge for some hierarchical dualistic theological interpretation. There are other ways of reading which make the story rather different, and these range from the priestly role of Mary, that is the one who 'activates' her son's redemptive power through her words and actions, to the divine marriage scenario mentioned earlier, with Mary, the mother, in the role of the great Mother goddess overseeing the wedding and ensuring that it provides the abundance that such a marriage of divinity was meant to provide. Either way, Mary the stooge has been transformed into a more proactive and powerful figure in the life of this story. Of course, body-theologian that I am, I am also content to read a story where a good party is being enjoyed by one and all. It is a reading that becomes possible if we dispense with the dualism and the metaphysics and engage with a man living and relating.

Much has been made of the other 'big Mary', Mary Magdalene, and her part in stories of resurrection. Once again it is possible to see her as a woman who misunderstood and who needed validation by the men. Mary finds an empty tomb and supposes the body has been moved, she tells Peter and then, when alone, she does not even recognize the man whom she has evidently loved for many years. Admittedly the Catholic Church did declare her apostle to the apostles because of her telling of this event, but again the tradition has in many ways failed to recognize her agency in that. She stumbled upon the truth through being led by the nose! However, many early feminist scholars enabled another reading of this story and I have been able to move from the forgiven sinner being a passive witness to viewing her as an insightful and passionate woman who could actually understand things at a deep and intuitive level – one who, precisely because of her outsider status, is just the right one to declare a radical message of counter-cultural living. It has also amused me over recent years to give up the reclamation that some scholars have attempted of her 'virtue'. What if she was a prostitute? What does that say about a movement that was funded by her work, as some contemporary scholarship suggests? To me this seems yet another interesting twist in an ever-changing tale!

And what of the sacraments that this Catholic theologian believed to be self-evident in John all those years ago? Well, a paradox. On the one hand this Gospel really does not have an advanced sacramental agenda – yes, a Last Supper but that may be it. Yet with a new understanding from feminist theology I am also tempted to look for more 'sacramental moments' in all of life and all the scriptures. In a world that is incarnational a few chosen actions are just not enough to express our deep connections between and within this web of human becoming. The liberation theologian also does not want to lose the powerful symbolism of a world eating together that may just be there in that Last Meal. We live in a world where more than half are starving and it seems as if the rest are dieting, so a non-dualistic engagement with this story may have something to challenge us with. Monica Hellwig argued that the way in which we view the 'hunger of the world' should always be within the context of the Last Supper which was, as she sees it, the foundational meal of Christianity. The context of this meal was one of oppression and the act of communal eating a commitment of ultimate fellowship – the sort that would be embodied through these continued acts of eating and radical praxis. I find myself reading the Johannine account as one in which what one ingested was the passion of Christ understood not as a final sacrifice but as a radical way of living counter-cultural praxis through the skin. Within the tension of realized eschatology in this book we may be able to say that we are fed with incarnation possibilities and sustained to ever widen the boundaries of this contained patriarchal order that does nothing to embrace and allow for the flourishing of our divine/human reality.

It is a traditional theological understanding among those from a high sacramental strand of Christianity to see connections between the feeding of the five thousand and the Last Supper. The former is seen to be a human precursor to the latter which is understood to be the ultimate metaphysical food, or so I was told at school. I now wish to see the connection lying in a radical commitment to feeding the world when we eat from that eucharistic table. The stories connect for me, not as a way to see what happens in the world as a sign for greater and 'more real' things beyond, but rather as a call to political action here and now. We live at a time when there is enough for each person on the planet to have 2,500 calories a day, in short, enough that no one need die from lack of food. This Johannine sacrament compels us to demand fairer production policies, better quality food, more equitable distribution and enough food on all tables, food that we eat with passion, with joy, with embodied pleasure. Some years ago, the theologian Tissa Balasuriya, in his book *The Eucharist and Human Liberation* (1979), urged Catholics to suspend the celebration of the Eucharist until such time as all were equal at the table. His argument was that around that table we proclaim the inclusion and equality of all in a world that in reality is unequal and excluding; his solution was then a suspension as a political act akin to individual hunger strikes in order to bring to the attention of global governments the need for radical change. A far cry from receiving metaphysical nourishment.

So now here I am, a feminist theologian, who has collapsed all the dualism that appears to be in John, who sees the 'sacramental' quality of that Gospel as political in nature and not ethereal, understanding very clearly the significance of food in this world – who controls it and who eats it. I attempt in my theology to let go in the way Jesus told Mary 'do not hold me' (John 20.17) while conveniently forgetting the second half of that verse 'for I have not yet ascended to the Father'. My letting go is in order to embrace the full becoming of the divine human person that I now think John 14.20 could refer to – a becoming that can not be accomplished if we cling to an outside hero, one who has done it all for us and requires nothing but faith and good actions. We have to embody the Christ we may profess to believe in, and the world of John may just allow for that. What it means is that there has as yet been no ascent to the Father. It remains outside my feminist imaginings and I would hope there would be no ascent to the Father again.

And I still live in the world where the time is coming and now is. That place where with the mystics we know, we feel, we grasp with the tips of our being that things can be different and we let go because the knowledge seems so fantastic to us – so out of this world yet rooted in it. It 'is coming' because we do not hold it but it 'now is' because we intuit it and feel it. I wonder then will quantum be the next step I take with John? Will this be a way to unlock some of the stranger sayings of that Gospel? Is quantum the place where the universes themselves and all they hold are collapsed into eternity which ever unfolds in each moment in creative and magical spiralling? Is quantum theology the language we have to stutteringly learn to speak? Will it be the language that in fact places us back in a world where 'transubstantiation' is accepted as the reality of life, the essence of our quantum existence and not a signal of dualistic hierarchy and a way to bridge the gap? I think we are moving to a place where embracing our *dunamis* allows us to know that reality is made and unmade, transformed in its essence by how we engage with it and act as the shape-shifters we are. Quantum theology is telling us that the fiery power of Tiamet is in our veins and the awesome, ever-changing paradoxical outpouring of generosity that enabled our initial being remains at the heart of each living thing.

We are creatures made from the stuff of the universe, our brains carry remnants of ancient mammalian structures, every fibre of our being is related to ancient bacteria and our ancestors are the stars. We are members of a symbiotic universe in which nothing stands alone and so, in short, we are creatures of belonging and relationality. Our alienation then from this process is entirely a fiction, there is no metaphysical world to protect us from the awesome reality of who we are. But what kind of belonging is this? It is belonging to creatively interacting systems, a network of interplay that moves always towards novelty woven from instability and an ever-moving universe. Not the kind of belonging that Christian theology has been used to with its Alpha and Omega point, the unchanging God, the same yesterday and tomorrow, the 'in the beginning was the Word' type! Indeed the One who remains ever constant for our sakes seems rather at odds with a universe that changes and does not have our interests at heart at all – that is to say it is not here for us, it exists for its own growth and becoming. What a strain this places on the once-and-for-all Christ and what power it lends to a religion that has incarnation at its heart. And what does it do to the Prologue in John? Well perhaps it makes a reading of cosmic beginnings possible without the power game of named origins. Edward Said reminds us that beginnings are always relative, contested and historical, whereas origins are absolute and power-laden. Beginnings then give the Christian theologian the chance to decolonize this space of origins in creation and the inevitable creator who sits apart and to challenge, as Catherine Keller has said, the great supernatural surge of father-power with a world appearing zap out of the void and mankind ruling the world in our manly creator's image. We are thrown back to cosmic beginnings, to void and chaos and we are asked to make our theology from that ground. To understand who we are and who we might be from *tohu vabohu*, the depth veiled in darkness. Once we give agency to void and chaos there can be no creation out of nothing as our power-laden dualistic origin. Creation ceases to be a unilateral act and the theological vista is cosmic! The divine speech in the pages of Genesis is no longer understood as a command uttered by the Lord and warrior King who rules over creation, but, as Keller prefers to think, 'let there be' is a whisper of desire and what comes forth emanates from all there is rather than appearing from above and beyond. In this shift we also see the possibility for incarnation to be understood as the rule rather than exception of creation because the whisper desires enfleshment. This Word of the Prologue then may become that whisper of desire uttered in the depth of time and the depth of our being: in the beginning was the power of our desire and it is made manifest out of love for the world, here and now. I seem to have moved a little since my convent days!

The Gospel of John is a book I do not read often but one that made a huge impression on me as a young girl and has been at the back, and often the front, of my mind ever since. It has moved from providing a cosmic frame in which to understand my existence, to being an illustration of how systems of power and privilege create the world we think we inhabit, and perhaps back to a more cosmic place but one hugely altered by a theo/political and quantum starting point. My eyes are fuller than they were at the time of my first reading of this book and my lived experience is allowed to play a much larger part than it ever was at the start. All of this makes this book very different from the code book for living that lay on the desk of that perplexed but eager to get it right 17-year-old 'A-level' student. It does feel to me that we, as a reading community, are on the edge of needing another language in order to understand the words we have in this book. Or perhaps we need to leave books such as this behind? Who knows? Ask me in ten years' time!

And did the author of John ever mean any of this – well, dear reader, that I cannot answer. We will all just have to keep living and reading! And, of course, I will have to keep facing the sticky bits that do not fit with any neat theories, be they feminist or otherwise, and still make this book a challenging read.

Reference

Tissa Ballasuriya (1979), *The Eucharist and Human Liberation*, London: SCM Press.

13

LOVE IN/OF THE BIBLE

Returning (to) Divine Love in the Book of Hosea

Yvonne Sherwood and Lesley Orr

This reflection on re-reading takes place between a book (the Bible and within it the book of Hosea), a biblical scholar (Yvonne Sherwood) and a feminist historian/activist currently developing the Scottish Government's Strategy to address Violence Against Women (Lesley Orr).

Yvonne Sherwood

Loving a book is such a familiar idea that it's become a cliché. Being loved by a book is more unusual – and perhaps more interesting. As a young girl growing up in a Protestant church, I was taught that I was loved by or through the book. The Book of Books, the Bible, was a divine statement of love addressed personally to me. Being divine, the love of God and God's Book was the love known as *agape*, not the lesser loves of *philia* or (worst of all) *eros*. The love of the Bible (with the Bible as subject, not object) was absolute, unselfish, superlative.

But not so much the other way round. In an illustration of the doctrine of original sin, no doubt, I found myself unable to reciprocate and give myself to the book as unreservedly as it gave itself to me. In all honesty, I had to confess I didn't really love the book, if loving the book meant being passionate about it, wanting to devour it or return to it again and again – or all those idioms that people use when they want to convey what it means to really love a piece of literature. In fact, my memory of childhood reading is a mixture of love and disappointment: loving reading, but often feeling disappointed with what I was reading. As a young girl in the 1970s, I was given far too many books about little girls whose heady ambitions extended so far as to enter a gymkhana or become a ballerina. But there seemed to be something supremely bad about being disappointed with the Bible. (I've since found that I was in good company, as such revered figures as St Augustine of Hippo felt similarly, before they learnt to re-read.)

Reading the Bible was bound up with obligation and the desire to be a good child. Though I read the Bible, it was the kind of reading in which I was acutely conscious of myself in the act of reading. I swallowed bits of Bible in chunks, like pills, in memory verses. And as I read the Bible I saw myself as the girl in a mental 'Picture of a Young (Good) Girl Poring Over Scripture'.

The first Children's Bible I remember was given to me by my grandfather for my seventh birthday, though he had died four days previously. The dedication was ghost-written by my mother. This gave that Bible an aura of double sanctity and double obligation. I read it to connect with someone now remote: the dead grandfather, whom I had loved, and not a million miles away in my symbolic universe, the (old man) God and his son who had given their book and life to me. I still have this version of the book (*The Hamlyn's Children's Bible in Colour*) in my office, and it occasionally weaves its way into the public (professional) discussions that I now have with the Bible. Its fabulous illustration of Jonah under what looks like a giant pumpkin, large enough to live in, found its way into my book on Jonah (Sherwood 2000, pp. 151–2). Looking at that picture again, I remember that I genuinely 'loved' the excessive bits that seemed very similar to fantasy and magic – though I was told that they belonged to the realm of miracle, which was an entirely different thing. The story of Elisha and the miraculous pot of oil was like the story of the magic porridge pot. Jonah's giant pumpkin pulled the sober-seeming Bible into the fantastic fairytale world of giant fruit and vegetables, such as Cinderella's pumpkin, Jack's beanstalk, and James' giant peach.

But what I genuinely loved were the dark and perplexing love bits that I only discovered when I began to read the uncensored Bible, the one used by adults. I loved the Gospel of John, Revelation, and above all the prophets. I was drawn to their strange language, awkward fragmentary phrases, outlandish metaphors, and the strange signs that the prophets made out of their own lives and bodies, as they obeyed commands to bury and retrieve a loin cloth, strip themselves naked, and marry an (the word had an aura of hazy naughtiness about it) 'adulteress'. Ezekiel in particular felt how I thought a Bible should feel: cryptic, strange, remote, holy. I loved the frisson of sacred mystery – but I also remember discovering, aged about 11, the dirty bits in Ezekiel 16 and 23 and feeling confused. It was an interesting experience – and one that seemed to place me confusingly between obedience and betrayal – to feel that I had inadvertently transgressed or stumbled across secret adult knowledge in the very act of obedient, good Bible reading.

I suspect that in many cases, and certainly in mine, the common memory of the simple, uncomplicated reading of the child is a nostalgic retrojection. I was easily bored by ponies and censored children's Bibles. I loved the dark and difficult bits of the Bible, Grimm's fairytales and older, undisneyfied forms of children's stories that initiate the child into the dark underside of the world. I've since read theories that suggest that the attraction of a good story is that it lets you experience danger and darkness in safety. The parts of the Bible that I loved were the ones that best offered this feeling of being safe in danger. Some of its passages made me feel the clash between safety and danger, being good and transgressing. And many of them took me vicariously into the darkest, bleakest scenarios from which I, the (loved and forgiven) reader, was saved.

The idea of the Bible that loved me, despite everything, was taught to me through two stories in particular: the prodigal son and its far less famous Old Testament counterpart, the book of Hosea, the only 'minor prophet' who got something of major billing. Hosea's wife, Gomer, like the prodigal son, was a useful visual aid for a certain kind of Protestant theology because she was the perfect image of the unlovable. As an adulteress, or harlot, she was the ultimate image of lack of virtue, or moral depravity – sin tending to find its most iconic expressions in the sexual (as opposed to, say, the social or economic). The book of Hosea was a divine tragedy, full of pathos, telling how the love of God was poorly reciprocated and betrayed – yet endured triumphant. God was the perfect husband and the perfect parent. The objects of his persistent love were the harlot running away with other gods and the young son ending up among the pigs. The two stories fitted well into the kind of Christianity that I came into contact with in my early teens, which was prone to extol the extreme conversion story. Stories of redemption from the depraved state of 'harlotry' or pig-swill were like biblical versions of the highly popular *Run Baby Run*, the story of the conversion of former New York gang leader Nicky Cruz. In the Christian circles I moved in during my late teenage years, the particular celebration of the black sheep regularly led to church-reared teenagers talking up past evils. It was not unusual to encounter Christians who had not yet reached their twenties but had already accrued implausible histories of sexual immorality or alcoholism.

In my early twenties, I took the book of Hosea through an unusually concentrated act of re-reading, when I started to read it for three years for my Old Testament/Hebrew Bible Ph.D. I didn't so much actively 'read against the grain' as begin to register thoughts that couldn't help but come to me from the late-twentieth-century context in which I was living. I'd never done this before, partly because of the sanctity that surrounds the Bible, forbidding public criticism, and partly because archaic words like 'harlotry' had kept the Bible apart in another, remote, biblical space, in a different world and a different vocabulary to the one in which I actually lived.

As soon as I started actively to read the book, I realized that it was full of shocking and transgressive pairings. Not only did a 'prophet' marry a 'prostitute', but pure *agape* was described in the language of *eros* and the God of love was highly anthropomorphized – jealous, coercive and violent. The husband, Hosea/God, threatened Gomer/the nation that he would 'strip her naked and expose her as in the day she was born, and take her into a wilderness . . . and kill her with thirst', 'hedge up her way with thorns and build a wall against her' and then 'allure her, and bring her into the wilderness, and speak tenderly to her' (Hosea 2.3, 6, 14) – the assumption being that she would eagerly return. This God who lurched from violence and control to excessive statements of love seemed to be modelled on the all-too-human form of what we would nowadays call an abusive partner: trapping his wife to keep her faithful, then stripping and humiliating her as punishment for perceived infidelity. The language could not be dismissed as safely metaphorical, because it slid between the metaphorical and the literal (a woman and a nation). It was, in a term that feminist biblical critics have since used, 'pornoprophetic'. The word may be new but it describes a phenomenon that I had been guiltily aware of in my childhood – though I had also learnt that identifying as a Christian involved learning to keep silent about the passages in the Bible (real) that seemed to betray 'the Bible' (ideal).

In my re-reading of Hosea the book remained a tragedy, but now from the perspective of God/Hosea's wife and children. The children, lurching between names like Loved and Not-Loved, looked like the unstable child who experiences love as deeply conditional and who searches for a stable image of love in the eyes of his/her parent. Once one's status has shifted from Not-Loved to Loved (Hosea 2.23) who is to guarantee that it will not tip back again? The harshness of the text's treatment of the woman/the nation seemed to backfire. Coercion and brutality graphically highlighted the limits of forms of theology that modelled monotheism on patriarchal monogamy. The text seemed to turn into an unwitting *justification* of what is seen as 'apostasy' insofar as it seemed to validate the attractiveness of 'other gods' or alternative visions of God. Though Gomer does not get to speak in her own voice in the text, I imagined that if she were to speak, God and Hosea (and the contemporary Church) might find some valid reasons why 'Gomers' have 'run away'.

Re-reading Hosea also taught me the necessity of identifying as a feminist. I became a feminist not by reading feminist criticism and theology (at least not at first) but by reading the Bible and commentaries on the Bible, which dissuaded me of my naively sanguine views of relative (and relatively liveable) equality. My first reaction to the text was not necessarily feminist – or only feminist in the most rudimentary sense. To feel queasy about images of a wife imprisoned, stripped, paraded and humiliated, you need not sign up to anything more progressive than the arguments of the suffragettes and campaigns against marital rape. Even more shocking than the biblical text itself was the treatment of Gomer in male-authored commentaries. Unlike the (male) prodigal, who tends to be treated with empathy and compassion as he sows his wild oats then eats them, Gomer is demonized and becomes the object of salacious speculation. In one theatrical version published in the 1920s she becomes a 'witch', a 'wild ape' and a monster, while male critics wax lyrical on the screams of Hosea, and the way the text breaks itself up into sobs. Revealingly, though the structure of the book's allegory places us, the reader, in the position of the sinful woman, commentators identify, to a man, with God and Hosea. In practice, the narcissistic tendencies of reading undercut the book's own allegory, with the male commentator finding himself comfortably on the side of God and the righteous husband. It seems to be a habit of reading – that easily transfers to the Bible – that we identify ourselves with the best characters and avoid the weakest position.

Over two and a half millennia later, the logic of the book of Hosea still feels current. The prophet (prophets being given to saying outrageous things) seeks to scandalize a male audience by saying 'You're a woman and you're a prostitute'. It seems that this statement is still so offensive that commentators (the professional readers who tell us how to read) find it impossible to identify with the sinful subject position.

Reflecting back on my first re-reading over ten years later, it now seems reminiscent of Anne Fadiman's account of re-reading C. S. Lewis's *The Horse and his Boy* with her son, and finding her beloved book guilty of misogyny and racism. She writes:

The problem with being ravished by books at an early age is that later rereadings are likely to disappoint . . . Your education becomes an interrogation lamp under which the hapless book, its every wart and scar exposed, confesses its guilty secrets. 'My characters are wooden! My plot creaks! I am pre-feminist, pre-deconstructivist, and pre-postcolonialist!' (The upside of English classes is that they give you critical tools, some of which are useful, but the downside is that those tools make you less able to shower your books with unconditional love. Conditions are the very thing you're asked to learn.) You read too many other books and the currency of each one becomes debased. (Fadiman 2005, p. xvi)

In my case I'd rewrite this. My re-reading articulated an equivocation I had felt before about the Bible, rather than betraying an unequivocal first love. My 'discovery' was rather that unconditional divine love was deeply conditional, in this text at least. The graphic sexual imagery made the very idea of being 'ravished' by the book deeply problematic. The biblical text was enriched, rather than debased, by being brought into contact with other literature. Gomer and her children, branded with the letter 'A', reminded me of Nathaniel Hawthorne's Hester Prynne in *The Scarlet Letter*. I liked the version of Gomer in the Christian poet Norman Nicholson's play *A Match for the Devil,* where Gomer teaches Hosea the true meaning of forgiveness, refusing to be a 'dirty cup to be rinsed out and set on the shelf again' while Hosea 'twiddles his magnanimous thumbs' (Nicholson 1953, p. 74).

For me, this example of re-reading would not be worth writing up if it were simple autobiography. What interests me about this first re-reading are the more general questions of conflict between the Bible and Modernity that it represents. I have recently realized that, far from doing something newly scandalous, feminist biblical critics like myself have been rediscovering and reinventing the old Enlightenment question of what I term *moral unbelief.* When we think about the modern Enlightenment critique of the Bible we tend to think rather rigidly of the separation between the Bible and fact or science. According to this oft-repeated version of European Modernity, the Bible's credibility came under fire when science led us to question accounts of demons, talking snakes and donkeys or reports of the sun standing still in the sky. As a reader of story, I've always felt this to be a non-problem, or, to put it another way, a question of genre. And now that I'm researching discussions of the Bible in seventeenth- and eighteenth-century Europe, I see that many thinkers in Germany and England were similarly unperturbed. What was important for them was the question of moral unbelief. Moral unbelief becomes possible when other sources of morality apart from the Bible come into existence and the Bible, viewed in the light of them, seems, in parts, morally dangerous or retrogressive. God's command to exterminate the Canaanites would be a case in point, and one to which these thinkers return again and again. If one strand of Enlightenment thought mocks the absurdity of biblical historicity, another, much heavier and generally earlier strand, agonizes over the *obligation* to criticize biblical texts on the grounds that signing up to them fully would involve the reader in the greater sin of moral unbelief.

I increasingly believe that it is crucial to revive this old question of moral unbelief – in biblical scholarship and in Church and Synagogue. This seems all the more pressing given the close relationship between these texts and actual bodies. If I were writing on Hosea again, I would want to supplement my first re-reading with a far greater consciousness of the relationship between textual violence and physical violence against women who are bound more closely than I ever was to the theologies and ideologies of these sacred texts. Intimate partner violence is gradually becoming a more visible issue in social policy (in schemes sponsored by the World Health Organisation and the Scottish Executive for example) and is no longer an entirely invisible issue in Christian contexts – though it still seems confined to fringe and pre-meetings of, say, the General Assembly of the World Council of Churches, and women who dare to voice accusations rarely receive a serious hearing. In mainstream Christian culture, the Christian critique of contemporary sexual issues seems obsessively directed at homosexuality and, to a lesser extent, (male) child abuse. Marriage still survives as the putative bastion of family values in the symbolic universe in which traditional readings of books like Hosea play a part. This lack of self-critique is shored up by the complacency of 'Western' culture, where the abuse and subordination of women tends to be seen as a retrogressive aberration of non-Christian, non-Western communities, epitomized in honour killings and the veil. For these reasons, I wanted to explore this question of re-reading Hosea in order to further upset the written canonical story with unwritten contemporary testimonies – which turn the book, once again, into the site of shocking 'revelation'. For this I turn to those who first made me aware of these stories – in particular my former colleague Lesley Orr.

Lesley Orr

A few years ago, as part of an action-research project about violence against women in Christian contexts, I invited a group of women to use clay to express their feelings about the abuse they had experienced. One (I'll call her Linda) constructed a very small space with very tall walls. The naked figure she moulded to represent herself was bowed, almost crushed, to fit inside, and was gagged with a scarf. She told the group that living with her violent husband had been like incarceration in a living tomb of fear, isolation, disorientation and suffocation. Her partner – a prominent and respected lawyer, and pillar of their local church – had employed a strategy of coercive and controlling behaviour which included habitual verbal abuse, pornographic degradation and occasional but severe physical brutality. He assumed the right to micro-regulate her life, so that she would perform to his satisfaction her designated roles as wife, mother, housekeeper and sexual partner, and provide the services to which he claimed entitlement as a man. He restricted her access to family, friends and workplace; to money and mobility. He told her what to wear and when. Occasionally he would lock her up in a cupboard for hours at a time, without clothes, food or drink. Their three children were implicated in the abuse – as witnesses, as bargaining counters, and encouraged by their father to subject her to insults. In a later interview, Linda told me:

I was so constricted, so fearful. I just lost myself really . . .
I wanted to try harder and harder all the time to be good,
to be a proper wife, to please him, to stop him hurting and
humiliating me. And the more I tried, the worse it got. There
was no 'I' left in the end – just a shadow fading into walls.

For 14 years, the husband told his wife and children that
everything he did was because he loved them, and 'for her
own good'. He claimed that without his regime of surveillance, regulation and control, his wife would revert to being
the whore and the slut who lurked dangerously in her breast: a
shameless bitch who would disgrace him in public and offend
his God-given role as husband and father.

As Linda spoke, and we looked at her figure walled up
and gagged, others in the group nodded in recognition. They
had similar stories of violation and entrapment at the hands
of Christian men and institutions, and in the name of love.
Jennifer, one of the women sitting round the table, stared at
the clay-walled enclosure and finally said, 'I've read your script
Linda – it's in the book of Hosea.'

I was a feminist who had received what purported to be the
best theological education the Scottish Education Department
could buy for me. That hadn't included anything about violence against women, or much about women at all actually,
though beyond the hallowed walls of New College I did read
about the biblical 'texts of terror'. But having grown up in local
church and family shaped by an Iona Community version of
the Christian story which was all about social justice and love,
I had never actually read the book of Hosea.

Jennifer, on the other hand, belonged to a church community which fervently adhered to the Truth of the Bible. She
had grown up with the practice of reading it from Genesis to
Apocalypse, beginning to end, and hearing sermons expound-
ing the Lord's will for his wayward people as revealed in stories
of murder and revenge, blood-lust and war, rape and torture,
sexual violence, submission and sacrifice. She had learnt that
whatever the text there was always a message: that God was
always good and in control; that the Word of God in the Good
Book had the power to scrutinize, judge and remake her sinful

self so that it would conform to his saving purpose. She found a copy of the Jerusalem Bible (we were in a Catholic retreat centre) and read the story of Hosea and Gomer. We listened to the language of masculine divine and human love:

Nothing but a whore
I make the House of Jehu pay
No more love . . . from me
Denounce your mother, denounce her
Let her rid her face of her whoring
Their mother has played the whore . . . has disgraced
    herself
I will display her shame
No one shall rescue her from my power
I mean to make her pay
Wall her in so that she cannot find her way
I am going to lure her
I will betroth you to myself forever, betroth you with
    integrity and justice, with tenderness and love
I bought her
You must keep yourself quietly for me
                                        (From Hosea 1 and 2)

The atmosphere in that room perceptibly tightened with stress and visceral fear as the group of women who were survivors of abuse (not just by partners, but by fathers, clergy, pimps, strangers and friends) heard these expressions of patriarchal intent and strategies for domination. The Hosea script was not just for Linda, but recognizable for them all. This was the language which had been utilized to dismantle their sense of personal integrity and worth, to disorientate, and to construct their identities as wicked girls, slags, bad mothers, provoking wives – and always, always whores. This was the language of seduction and punishment, possession and control. And it was, according to the Good Book, the language of love. Jennifer told us that when she was a young woman, she heard a sermon praising Hosea 1—3 as 'one of the great love stories of all time'.

For most of the women gathered around the table, one way

and another, love stories like that had scripted the dynamics of the abuses to which they had been subjected. They were, to use Yvonne's phrase, 'loved by the Bible'. It gave them a story to live by, a pious language about authority and purpose and forgiveness; but it shut them up – kept quiet by what one woman described as a tyranny of holy respectability, and deprived of the resources they needed to recognize, name and disclose the injustice and malevolence visited upon them by men: men who mostly assumed a God-given right to mould women (as God had created the derivative and ancillary Eve) as 'vessels for use'.

All over the world, the usefulness of girls and women to the hegemonic projects of personal, social, economic and political mastery (or to put it more theoretically, the co-existing feudal, modern and postmodern gender orders) constrains and compromises facile assumptions of equality and human rights. This notion has provided fertile ground for pervasive gender-based violence, not as some kind of aberration (committed by the monsters and sex beasts beloved of our salacious press), but as the everyday context in which female human beings are born, grow up and have to learn how to be 'women'.

Imagine a people routinely subjected to assault, rape, sexual slavery, arbitrary imprisonment, torture, verbal abuse, mutilation, even murder – all because they were born into a particular group. Imagine further that their sufferings were compounded by systematic discrimination and humiliation in the home and workplace, in classrooms and courtrooms, at worship and at play. Few would deny that this group had been singled out for gross violations of human rights . . .

Such a group exists. Its members comprise half of humanity. Yet it is rarely acknowledged that violence against women and girls, many of whom are brutalized from cradle to grave simply because of their gender, is the most pervasive human rights violation in the world today. (Bunch 1997)

It has been a great achievement of feminism to name and to politicize this hidden epidemic. My own involvement in the movement can be traced back 30 years to a defining moment in my life. I was working for a church-sponsored youth project, and living in a (long-since demolished) council flat in Glasgow. One Saturday night I looked out of the window and saw my neighbour being dragged by her hair along the street by her husband. He kicked and screamed at her: 'You're a fucking whore, bitch.' Ruchill was a place where violence often erupted into public space, but this performance made me feel really frightened and angry. I did nothing, although the next day I spoke to the woman about what had happened and she simply said, 'Och, it's just the way things are.' But she also told me that her priest had given her some advice that she took to heart: she had made her bed, now she would just have to lie on it, because marriage was a holy sacrament, and God wanted her to forgive and try harder to please her husband. (These words, I later discovered, spookily echoed a letter written by Calvin about a Genevan woman abused by her husband: 'she must bear with patience the cross which God has seen fit to place upon her, and meanwhile not to deviate from the duty which she has before God to please her husband, but to be faithful whatever happens' (quoted in Watt 1993): a fine example of ecumenical concord.)

This advice seemed so wilfully dangerous and disempowering, so ignorant and inhumane, that I could not understand how it could emanate from a representative of Christianity, which I thought was at heart a story of justice, compassion and fullness of life. What kind of God would demand such counsel in the name of love? Since then, I've been involved in activism, advocacy, education, campaigning and research on the violation of women's safety, rights and autonomy: trying to understand 'the way things are'; hearing and telling alternative stories which say the way things are is not the way things have to be.

This is not the place for information or analysis. There is a mountain of research and literature and declarations and policies and strategies devoted to describing, examining and seeking to prevent gender-based violence in all its depressingly diverse but entirely functional variations. In some societies, the superior status and privilege of men and the inferior, circumscribed position of women is enshrined and supported in law and politics. In others, including our own, the norms and regulations which for centuries institutionalized inequality have been contested and adjusted. Since the 1960s, the pace of social and legal change has accelerated, and alternative discourses of gender relations based on equality, mutuality, respect and choice have challenged the rigidity of stereotypes about the roles and expectations of women and men. But notions of male entitlement – especially around provision of domestic and sexual services – remain surprisingly widespread and resilient. Such ideas receive powerful cultural support, not least from the hugely profitable and proliferating global traffic and consumption of women in pornography and prostitution, and for domestic labour or as 'mail order brides'. This is the bright new dawn of a supposedly post-feminist world. In all social contexts of inequality – including intimate relationships – intimidation and physical force (and the threat of such violence) has been a resource used to impose or reinforce power. It may not always be necessary actually to engage in violent acts, if other mechanisms of power are available and effective. But in family life, as in colonization or national aggrandizement, such acts have been justified as legitimate means to maintain dominance and privilege.

The economic and social costs of violence against women are enormous, but they should not obscure the profoundly harmful impact on the personal health, wellbeing and sense of self for millions upon millions of girls and women. Fullness of life? From my vantage point that sounded like a cruel joke, and I wanted to know why my religious tradition had been complicit in creating cultures, traditions and leadership which commonly supported the subordination and violation of women. I had a hunch that it was to do with the power of stories, and in particular with divine authorization of 'The Story' apparently contained in the Book of Books. Since my Ruchill epiphany, I have encountered and listened to many women within Christian traditions, from all over the world, talking about the ways that their lives have been shaped in the context of a faith community which canonized the Bible and filtered women's perceptions of themselves through the lens, as Delores Williams has put it, of 'a male story populated by human males, divine males, divine male emissaries, and human women mostly servicing male goals' (Williams 1993, p. 1987). When I conducted research interviews with women in Scotland who were survivors of personal and institutional abuse in church contexts, I was perplexed to discover that so many of their narratives were fashioned by a deep sense of shame which interpreted and sustained their violation as something they deserved, or provoked, for failing to be 'good' women – or simply for being born female, and hence culpable. 'I felt guilty because somehow I had failed to conform to the image of Christian wife and mother and that certainly added to the isolation . . . I was shamed into silence.'

I am not claiming that there is a direct correlation between religious belief or practice, and the prevalence of violence against women. This is a complex variable, and recent research suggests that in some social contexts there may be evidence of salutary or protective effects. I do know from my own research and from my work with the World Council of Churches that very many women who experience abuse indicate that their personal faith and religious involvement are significant if not fundamental factors in attempts to give meaning to their experiences, to make decisions and to seek support and advice. In many situations faith is an important resource for sanctuary and resistance against dehumanization.

But if the Bible is read as divine revelation, in a community which interprets those texts as evidence that the God of love sometimes acts (and is entitled to act) like a jealous, wilful and controlling husband within a kinship system based on honour and shaming, how does that impact on abused women? To say the least, they struggle with a discourse – a dominant grand narrative – which seems to provide divine validation of that abuse from the perspective of the perpetrator: a perspective they are likely already to have internalized and made their own. It doesn't help if the self-blame and shame is reinforced by the attitudes and actions of the faith community which tells The Story – and that has been the wounding reality for countless survivors of gender violence. For years, Linda, Jennifer and other women I know accepted their naming and treatment as sinful women, deserving of insult, abuse, control and punishment. They concurred with the judgement of the text, of commentators, of those with power in their churches, and accepted at face value their identification with the rebellious harlots and wicked wives. So despite their best efforts to be true to the Christian ethics of love, they were persuaded that it was they who needed to repent, be rescued and remade in conformity with that divine love which has proved such a useful accomplice to controlling men. If the story women have learnt to live by depends on their being nice, helpful, accommodating, polite, dutiful, respectable; if it has taught them that their own value is associated almost entirely with the satisfaction of the needs and desires of others; if it has encouraged them to trust and obey men in positions of authority, the consequences can be devastating. One of the women I interviewed had been sexually abused by her minister:

> He used to say it was God's will, and that he was God's representative. I had grown up being told to obey the will of God. I was so confused. For years I didn't call it abuse, but I knew it had harmed me. I knew HE had harmed me, betrayed my trust, exploited my vulnerability. I was expected to absorb it, to take the blame for it and to keep quiet about it. The whole situation when I look back on it now was disgusting. It makes me so angry, because my faith had conditioned me to allow powerful men to define what I was, so for years I had no resources for resistance. It took me years when I really felt like I was burning in hell, before I got that man and his hideous god out of my body and out of my life.

Is this hideous god any use as a source of safety, compassion or empowerment for women enduring violation? And whose interests are served if we keep returning to ancient accounts of his authorized domination with some kind of obligation to extract 'messages' about divine love and purpose? This is a deeply untrustworthy and, as Yvonne suggests, an unethical enterprise. Plenty of resilient and resourceful women have devoted enormous intellectual and emotional energy to developing feminist reading strategies – rooting around against the grain or as cunning tricksters to find cleverly subversive sub-texts to the Master plan. As one feminist poet and literary critic has said, 'I strive for healing and so must confront what is toxic' (Ostriker 1993, p. 30). But is there not a case for toxic waste disposal? Instead of devoting energy wrestling counter-intuitively to find constructive readings of texts like Hosea, might we not simply remove their authority, both practically and symbolically, from lives and communities, and take them or leave them as literature? The Bible (or more precisely, the interpreting communities which make privileged claims for its disparate but closed collection of texts as self-evident, normative sources of inspiration and guidance for our lives) sometimes exercises a regime of coercive control akin to that practised by men who place women under regulation and surveillance, and who punish non-compliance. Women often find creative and courageous ways to cope and survive under such a regime: anticipation, diversion, secret mockery of power, and undermining of rules. But these strategies are rarely transformative of the regime itself, or the abusive power relations thereby exercised. And what's more, they perpetuate one of the most tenacious characteristics of its logic: that those who are violated and colonized also carry the burden of responsibility for understanding and making the relationship 'work'. They are expected to deal with dissonance: to change their story, their identity, their sense of what is just and right, to make it fit with the perspective and demands of the master's story.

Central to the personal and political struggle against abuse of power is asserting the right to cast off that burden and claiming the right to say that the master's story is both dangerous and wrong. Breaking the silence is an act of rupture to lay bare institutional collusion and to rebel against those texts utilized in defence of morally reprehensible purposes. From this standpoint (it may be the silenced Gomer's) it is liberating to embrace the full implications of biblical identification as a whore and choose to apostasize from belief in the posing, plotting patriarchal god. To re-read in this case may be to no longer read. It may prove deeply necessary to betray the Bible – or at least reciprocate with conditional love.

References

C. Bunch (1997), 'The Intolerable Status Quo: Violence Against Women and Girls', in *The Progress of Nations*, New York: UNICEF.

J. Calvin (1993), Letter from Calvin to Mme de Grammont, 28 October 1559, quoted in Jeffrey Watt, 'Women and the Consistory in Calvin's Geneva', *Sixteenth Century Journal* 24:2, pp. 429–39.

A. Fadiman (ed.) (2005), *Rereadings: Seventeen Writers Revisit Books They Love*, New York: Farrar, Strauss and Giroux, p. xvii.

N. Nicholson (1953), *A Match for the Devil*, London: Faber & Faber.

A. S. Ostriker (1993), *Feminist Revision and the Bible*, Oxford: Blackwell.

Y. Sherwood (2000), *A Biblical Text and Its Afterlives: The Survival of Jonah in Western Culture*, Cambridge: Cambridge University Press.

Y. Sherwood (2004), *The Prostitute and the Prophet: Rereading Hosea in the Late Twentieth Century*, New York: Continuum.

D. Williams (1993), *Sisters in the Wilderness: The Challenge of Womanist God-Talk*, Maryknoll: Orbis.

Lightning Source UK Ltd.
Milton Keynes UK
03 November 2009
145751UK00001B/40/P